THE ULTIMACY OF JESUS

Aureus Studies in Post-Foundational Theology

This series aims to articulate a new and developing approach to the relationship between the Christian tradition and contemporary culture. Rather than seeing this as a clash between metanarratives each built upon firm and incontrovertible foundations the various texts explore the possibilities for a relationship between traditions more guarded and humble in their claims to truth. This does not mean that the frameworks and assumptions are no longer of any value but that they need to be treated as contingent and provisional. This approach has a particular significance for practical engagement, whether pastorally, politically or socially based and is thus of value for developing a public theology at a time when Christianity's credibility outside its own boundaries is in considerable doubt.

Other books in the series:

Beyond All Reason: The limits of post-modern theology
John Reader, 1997
ISBN 1-899750-02-9

Agape, moral meaning and pastoral counselling
Simon Robinson, 2001
ISBN 1-899750-09-6

Truth and Scripture: Challenging underlying assumptions
Brenda Watson, 2004
ISBN 1-899750-27-4

Blurred Encounters: A reasoned practice of faith
John Reader, 2005
ISBN 1-899750-35-5

All published by Aureus Publishing Limited

THE ULTIMACY OF JESUS

The Language and Logic of Christian Commitment

Trevor Williams

AUREUS

First published in 2009 by
Aureus Publishing Limited

© 2009 Trevor Williams

All rights reserved. No part of this publication may be reproduced, stored in a retrieval system, or transmitted, in any form or by any means, electronic, mechanical, photocopying, recording or otherwise, without the prior permission of the publisher.

ISBN 10: 1-899750-42-8
ISBN 13: 978-1-899750-42-9

A catalogue record for this book is available from the British Library.

Typeset by Andrew Buckley, Clunton, Shropshire.

Printed and bound in Great Britain by Athenaeum Press Ltd.

Aureus Publishing Limited
Castle Court
Castle-upon-Alun
St Bride's Major
Vale of Glamorgan
CF32 0TN

Tel: 01656 880033
International Tel/Fax: (+044) 1656 880033

E-mail: sales@aureus.co.uk
Website: www.aureus.co.uk

To Rebecca and Catherine

Contents

Acknowledgements	xi
Introduction	1
1. Pluralism and Personhood	7
2. The enrichment of sacrifice	31
3. Redemption and reconciliation in Christ	49
4. The trouble with the Resurrection	71
5. The Lordship of Christ and the language of Ultimacy	87
6. Faiths in the light of the Christian Faith	137
7. Conclusion	153
Appendix: The doctrine of the Trinity as the foundation of the Christian faith	155
Bibliography	161
Index of modern authors	167
General index	169

Acknowledgements

I would particularly like to thank my friend and former student, Andrew Buckley, for doing the typesetting with painstaking attention to detail and with helpful comments on the content. My thanks are also due to the students and colleagues, too many to mention individually, who over many years have stimulated discussion and challenged my ideas. Where I have gone wrong I have only myself to blame.

Introduction

Over many years of teaching theology I have had occasion to address a great variety of issues in lectures, articles and sermons. Despite their diversity, a connecting thread runs through them, namely, the question of ultimacy. The term echoes Paul Tillich's use of the expression 'ultimate concern' to speak of God, and I readily admit to Tillich's influence on my own thinking, but not, I hope, in slavish dependence.[1]

The particular question addressed here is, What does it mean to proclaim the ultimacy of Jesus of Nazareth and how can this be expressed in the light of a contemporary scientific understanding of the world, in the context of religious and cultural pluralism, and not least in the face of widespread misunderstanding (if not culpable ignorance), of how commitment to Jesus Christ can be maintained without sacrificing intellectual integrity or lapsing into fundamentalism. It may be noted that fundamentalism is certainly not the exclusive preserve of religions. It rears its ugly head in extreme forms of secularism, scientism, and in ideologies of various kinds that ostensibly have no place for God or religion but yet lay claim to the ultimate truth of existence.

Another crucial question to be faced today is whether the very idea of anything being ultimate is not only misguided but dangerous. Even if it survives the critiques of postmodernism, can it escape the charge of fomenting conflict? At a time when our world is riddled with fundamentalisms of various sorts, many would argue that the only way to maintain peace and good relations is to surrender all claims to ultimacy and to acknowledge only the relative value of different religions and traditions.

There is much to be said for this irenic approach. It can be illustrated by the frequent allusions these days to the Abrahamic religions: Judaism, Christianity, and Islam, which all acknowledge Abraham as their common ancestor. It's true, they do, and this approach may well serve the cause of peace by promoting mutual respect and goodwill. For that it is to be welcomed, but wittingly or unwittingly, it may serve to elevate Abraham as the ultimate and as a result relativize all three historical faiths. For many of their adherents this is too high a price to pay, even if the price of not paying it may be conflict. By definition there can only be one ultimate, just as for monotheists there can only be one God. Hence we find the adherents of different ultimates all claiming more or less aggressively to occupy the moral, religious and theological high ground, and all equally sure that God is on their side (even to the point of suicide and murder in his name).

The question of ultimacy is the proper concern of religion, which cannot be satisfied with being regarded merely as a cultural phenomenon (where diversity can of course be accepted without much difficulty). One might say that it is passion or at least concern for the ultimate that marks out the religious person from society at large. Inasmuch as it is a passion for truth or for what is ultimately real and good, it may be hailed as a virtue. At the same time the passion for the ultimate (for the truth, for God) is what makes religious people so dangerous.

To put it simply, it is those who care most about God who are at greatest risk of mistaking what is not quite God for God, that is, they risk attaching ultimacy to the wrong thing, something less than ultimate (in traditional language, idolatry). The result, in Tillich's terms, is to unleash the demonic, that is, the destructive power that results from treating what may be and often is a limited or partial good in itself as the ultimate good. This is all too likely to provoke in turn an angry backlash from competing claims to possess the truth.

This understandable but nevertheless disastrous outcome can occur in any religion, not excluding Christianity. The risk is greatest when a religion or any claim to ultimacy is threatened or under attack. In a fearful defensive reaction it is then all too likely that religions or their adherents will assert the absolute, ultimate authority of their particular claim to truth. However, it's important to recognize that short of the extremes of idolatry, there may be a tendencies towards over-valuation which, once identified, can be resisted. This can result in the recovery of the true value, not the destruction, of what has been overrated.

Such problems can arise within Christianity, as some examples from the Roman Catholic and Protestant churches may illustrate. In both there are those who sincerely acknowledge the ultimacy of Jesus and who try to live lives inspired by him, but who implicitly or explicitly maintain the ultimacy of their particular response, for example, their particular church. This claim may be expressed politely and even sympathetically, but nevertheless by its own logic it is bound to deny equal value to alternative responses to Jesus, and may even lead to the repression or persecution of others.

Introduction

The situation can be illustrated by the ambivalent attitude towards ecumenism to be found in various churches and denominations. Ecumenism tends to provoke anxious suspicion since it seems to (and in fact does) relativize the claims of different churches to be the true upholders of the ultimacy of Jesus. So though Pope Benedict XVI's claim that the Roman Catholic Church is the only true church is understandable, it outrages members of other Christian churches who, though certainly respecting the witness to Jesus of the Roman Catholic Church, would nevertheless deny its ultimacy.[2] (To extend the principle of ecumenism to embrace other communities of faith is liable to generate even greater concern).

On the other side, the professed defenders of Biblical faith are all too often in practice demanding the acceptance of a particular literalistic reading of the Bible (which would probably amaze the original authors, not least the author of the Book of Revelation!). They make this the central focus of commitment. Thus instead of locating the ultimate in the order and being of the Church, they locate it in the Scriptures. The infallibility of the Pope is countered by the infallibility (or inerrancy) of the Bible.

The situation is highly complex and individuals may find themselves at various points on the spectrum between Church or Bible. Often for Christ's sake they may simply choose to live with unresolved tensions, such as when a Pope kneels beside an Archbishop of Canterbury before the altar in Canterbury cathedral[3] and yet is officially bound to reject the validity of Anglican orders, while his successor denies that the Anglican Church is truly a church at all. Meanwhile Anglicans themselves divide over the claims to ultimacy made for the Bible or tradition.

This situation cannot or at least should not be allowed to persist. The unresolved tensions are all too often the product of questionable assumptions treated as absolutes. As such they implicitly undermine the ultimacy of Jesus and are liable to raise unnecessary intellectual and moral obstacles to commitment to him. To take an example from the Roman Catholic Church again, it is well known for its uncompromising opposition to abortion, and yet is equally opposed to the use of contraception which could prevent or at least reduce the demand for abortion while helping to reduce widespread poverty and to protect against the horror of AIDS. If the ultimacy of the Church could more readily be questioned, the possibility of mistakes in its understanding and teaching could more easily be admitted and more positive and creative responses to advances in knowledge could be entertained.

Inroduction

Two major issues now confronting Christians of all persuasions relate to creation and human sexuality. In the former case the tragedy is that those who insist, and require others to insist, on a literal reading of Genesis are creating a gulf between Christians and ordinary people who acknowledge the validity of the current scientific view of the world (while admitting that scientists can be wrong and don't have all the answers). Uncritical literalism will give rise to a kind of ghetto theology, practised by a self enclosed group whose members (like Scientologists) can talk with each other but not with the world outside, the world lived in by most people. To proclaim the ultimacy of Jesus on these terms is to deny his ultimacy in the real world and to affirm it in a make-believe world based on a misconstruction of the Biblical message.[4] At the same time, a literalistic interpretation of scripture offers those who deny the ultimacy of Jesus an easy target for their scorn and so paradoxically hampers the mission of the Church rather than advancing it.

The case of homosexuality and other moral issues will not be pursued further here except with the observation that underlying them usually are sincere but deeply divergent convictions over the Bible and tradition. The challenge for Christians is whether the passionate appeal of Paul to uphold the unity of the Church is compatible with the divisions that have arisen within it.

Although the contents of this book originated in different times and places, they are linked together in so far as they can be seen to express the ultimacy of Jesus. This is the issue that is examined here in relation to the traditional doctrines of incarnation, sacrifice, redemption, resurrection, the Trinity, and finally in relation to other faiths.

The first chapter engages with the critical question of what it means to be a person, and how our way of thinking about persons today may bear on the person of Jesus if we take his humanity seriously. It also reflects on how his way of being a person may bear on the way we can be persons today. The second chapter explores the way the language of sacrifice came to be used and understood, and how it could serve to express the ultimacy of Jesus if his death is seen to be sacrifice and not punishment. This leads on in the third chapter to an inquiry into the life transforming impact of Jesus on his followers, then and now, in terms of what he turned them away from (sin, the devil, the demonic, idolatry) and what he turned them towards (the new vision and experience of God imparted by Jesus' life and death). That brings us in the fourth chapter to the fundamental and yet daunting question of Jesus' resurrection. What really happened? How is it to be understood? At

Introduction

least one implication of the resurrection and ascension of Jesus was and is his exaltation to ultimacy. The question then is how is he to be understood in relation to the ultimate, that is, to God? And how is God to be understood in relation to the ultimacy of Jesus and in relation to the Holy Spirit?

The way the early church wrestled with these issues, and its struggle to find the right language to express its faith in the ultimacy of Jesus, is explored in the longest chapter here.[5] The question then to be faced is whether the doctrine of the Trinity is an outdated metaphysical irrelevance, part of a great delusion, or whether it is truly the only, or at least the best, way to undergird the ultimacy of Jesus. Tradition would claim the latter, but the question arises whether the doctrine of the Trinity is non-negotiable or is it now in fact a major but unnecessary obstacle to faith and to good community and inter-faith relations? That issue is investigated further in the last chapter. A brief summary and positive statement of the Trinitarian doctrine is included in an appendix.

These are the issues explored in the following pages. It will be argued that the language of the Bible and tradition may be best understood as *expressing* ultimacy rather than *describing* it. I will try to show how in different contexts and in response to different questions, every kind of resource was harnessed by Jesus' early followers to express his ultimacy, but the question remains, Can this response to Jesus any longer be justified?

Many would say 'No', but if the answer is 'Yes', a fundamental question arises, namely, What must reality as such be like for it to be possible for that particular human being, Jesus from Nazareth, to be ultimate in fact, and not merely in human imagination or as a social projection? In somewhat technical terms, What is the ontological corollary (or precondition) of the confession, 'Jesus is Lord'? This is where the question of God can be properly addressed, as it arises out of the ultimacy of Jesus, rather than as a preconceived idea to which Jesus must be conformed. Thus the question still remains, What is the reality to which the symbol, 'God', is pointing? Is there really any such reality?

So we come to the age old question, 'Does God exist?'. Too often it is treated in isolation as a logical plaything and argued *ad nauseam* with little advantage to those engaged with it. But in so far as it arises out of the question of the ultimacy of Jesus, we are justified in concentrating on this foundation, without at this point having to pursue all the wide ranging theological and moral implications that follow from it. The basic question remains, Is Jesus ultimate? Is he worthy of our ultimate commitment? Is the definitive clue to ourselves, our world, and our destiny to be found in him

Inroduction

and his story rather than anywhere else or in anyone else? – to believe this to be so is in no way to deny the courage and Christ-like saintliness of many who have not heard of Jesus or responded to him; nor is it to disparage the great traditions of faith in which millions of human lives have been nurtured. It is to set out on a path mapped by Jesus of Nazareth, however much we stumble and fall in our attempts to follow him.

I write as an unrepentant liberal theologian who believes that the truth of Christianity does not rest on belief in a literalistic interpretation of scripture or on the binding authority of traditional doctrinal formulations or on any single human being since Jesus himself. But however sincerely these beliefs are held, sincerity is no substitute for truth, and that must apply to all of us. At heart, despite the diversity of language and practice, and the objections which may be raised, Christian discipleship is commitment to the ultimacy of Jesus, whatever language we may use to express it and whatever action it demands.

It is obviously impossible to deal adequately with such big issues within the compass of this small book, but it may serve to shed some light and, perhaps, to remove at least some unnecessary obstacles to commitment to Jesus. It may thus open the way to non-Christians as well as Christians to discover the exciting and creative possibilities for life and understanding that may arise from critical engagement with the Bible and tradition and above all from the picture of Jesus that emerges from them.

Jesus himself remains elusive, but not wholly inaccessible. There is enough given for commitment to Jesus to be a rational and realistic decision, and enough hidden to prevent misguided over confidence in one's own experience and understanding of the ultimacy of Jesus. .

I turn now to some of the different ways in which this has found expression, beginning with the way the ultimacy of Jesus may bear on the lives of human persons.

Notes

1 For a brief note about Tillich, see p. 142 below.

2 'The Vatican has described the Protestant and Orthodox faiths as "not proper Churches"...' Roman Catholicism was 'the one true Church of Christ'. Statement from the Congregation of the Faith. Reported in The Times, 11 July 2007.

3 Pope John Paul II and Archbishop Robert Runcie on 29 May 1982.

4 Creation science is a contradiction in terms, since however skilfully (and sometimes even illuminatingly) empirical evidence is handled, it is, unlike true science, bound to one predetermined outcome.

5 A revised version of chapter 7 in my book *Form and Vitality in the World and God* (Oxford 1985).

1

PLURALISM AND PERSONHOOD[1]

Before considering the ultimacy of the historical person, Jesus, it would seem appropriate to address the basic question, What does it mean to be a person? This question underlies all discussion concerning human aspirations, values and ideas of fulfilment, and yet it cannot easily be answered. The sheer variety of human life, religion, and culture raises two further questions. First, is there any unifying factor underlying the diversity, one that can still justify the idea of a common humanity (and so of course, of human rights)? This seemingly obvious concept has not only been threatened in theory by the forces of postmodernism, but has been violently abrogated in practice in Bosnia, Rwanda, and elsewhere in the world. Secondly, and closely related to the first question, Can there be any valid way of evaluating different belief systems and modes of human self-actualization which is not arbitrary, judgemental, or imperialistic? Or must any attempt at critical evaluation of what it is to be human simply be abandoned, leaving the field to a kind of spiritual apartheid, separate developments that cannot be connected or reconciled? These are the issues I wish to explore in this chapter.

Just how unclear the notion of personhood can be was highlighted in a newspaper report a few years ago:

> A witness in a bizarre trial in Wisconsin has been sworn in three times so far, once for each of her multiple personalities who have so far testified. Psychiatrists say that another 43 personalities inhabit the woman's body, and they may yet have also to be sworn in, including one which is described as 'having evolved from a small animal which lives beneath tables and growls when frightened'.[2]

The phenomenon of multiple personality is not new to psychology, of course. Though it sounds amusing, it is a tragic condition, often related to childhood abuse. The goal of treatment is the integration of the many personalities. My point with this quotation is not to pursue that problem

Chapter 1

but to underline two things, first, that the intuitive sense of being one person, more or less, is not automatic or a guaranteed feature of human life; it may be that becoming a person is a more hazardous project than many suppose. Secondly, despite all the problems, it is generally assumed in our society that to be an integrated person is a good thing, and that the condition of multiple personality is one that needs healing.[3]

However, a case might be made that, so far from being a psychological aberration, multiple personality or even non-personality may be a natural state of affairs. Or to put it differently, what our culture reacts against as a problem to be corrected, may be positively reinforced in another culture as the proper way of being human. The question then arises as to whether we have the right to suppose that our understanding and experience of being persons is universally valid or even valid at all. There are those who argue that not only God, but our very selves are product of social constructions or projections, that is, the creations of different societies and not real in themselves. Feuerbach[4] marches on! It is this new challenge to Christian Anthropology posed by Social Constructionists that I wish to explore here, with particular reference to Rom Harré and Jeroen Jansz.[5] I will begin with a summary of their ideas about persons and selves, and will then explore the implications for an understanding of Jesus, and vice versa (i.e. the implications of a Christian understanding of Jesus for Social Constructionist theories, with reference to Alistair McFadyen's thorough treatment of the subject).[6] I will argue that ideas of selfhood and personhood are closely correlated with ideas of God, and that pluralism in the one case is likely to be matched by pluralism in the other. I will conclude that pluralism has its place in the realm of the penultimate, but that radical pluralism must be resisted not only for God's sake but for the sake of humanity.

It has of course long been recognized that human beings understand themselves in many different ways, from the Biblical view of psychosomatic body-soul unity, to the Greek dualist view of body and soul as essentially distinct. The debate continues between Cartesians and their opponents, between Richard Swinburne and Richard Strawson, and with scientists such as Francis Crick and Richard Dawkins. On a different front Christians affirm selfhood in some sense, while Buddhists treat the self as ultimately illusory.

Despite the variations, it has generally been supposed that what is true for one human being is true for all. In the West most would suppose that even if the sense or experience of one's self was not quite the same as other people's, at least one had a 'self'. The 'inner me' or 'I' of identity has been conceived of as a fundamental reality that survives through bodily and psychological change (and perhaps even death). It is these assumptions that are now being questioned. It is argued that neither Buddhist views nor Western views in all their diversity are applicable to all, because none is universally valid – the self, it is argued, is neither illusory nor a substantial entity, but an organizing 'theory' that is indispensable in our particular moral order, but not in others. 'Paradoxically, it is only by believing in such an inner active core of self that *our* psychological attributes and *our* moral order can be realized.'[7] Thus Harré speaks of personal being as 'contingent',[8] or treats 'the sense of self as a local contingency'.[9] If the self, or 'self-narrative' in Jansz's terms,[10] is a contingent construct, it would seem that nothing remains in common between all human beings except the physiological and the neurological conditions that make theoretical constructs possible.

The Social Constructionist case is that personhood, or selfhood, is not something given at birth, nor is it an innate quality that develops automatically like the appearance of a beard on the face of a youth, nor indeed is it any *thing* substantial. Rather it is a possibility one may or may not be given or respond to, a project to be pursued or abandoned. Existentialists could agree that 'the essence of man is not to be but to become.' The big question is, Become what? This, according to Social Constructionists, is far from being a matter of personal decision. The crucial first steps are taken before we are capable of decision, in infancy, and may lead in very different directions. To quote John Shotter, 'Human beings have no personal powers at birth at all; they only gain these in negotiated interaction with those who already possess them,'[11] which is his way of saying that a baby becomes a person through being treated as a person by its parents. Jansz makes a similar point when he says 'being addressed as 'you' is crucial for the development of personhood;'[12] so also Harré when he speaks of the mother's role in creating a person 'by treating a merely animate being as such.'[13] In effect, Mums and Dads are person-makers, 'No empirical discovery of an inner self is even hinted at.'[14]

The distinction to be drawn between 'person' and 'self' is important though not always clearly sustained by different authors. Harré defines persons as 'social individuals ... identifiable by public criteria.' By contrast, 'selves are psychological individuals, manifested in the unified organization of perceptions, feelings and beliefs of each human being who is organized in that fashion in their own regard.' He goes on to say that 'the basic thesis of [his] work is that animate beings are persons if they are in possession

Chapter 1

of a theory – a theory about themselves,' and later, 'the self is a theoretical concept by which we organize our experience into unities.'[15] Jansz describes personhood as 'the public conception of the individual human being' which can be partially internalized. 'This private conception can be called selfhood.'[16]

Thus (following Harré) person-makers – Mums and Dads – communicate through 'conversational practices', or 'person-engendering language games', a theory to 'an animate being who is thereby transformed into a person'. These crucial language games take place in conditions of 'psychological symbiosis'. 'One who is always presented as a person [e.g. by the mother], by taking over the conventions through which this social act is achieved, becomes organized as a self.'[17]

In other words, persons, publicly locatable human beings within a moral order, impart a theory of self to an animate being. By internalizing it, the animate being is able to organize its experiences in such a way as to manifest itself publicly as a person. 'The very possibility of personal being depends on the existence of selves as the modes of the organization of experience...'[18] An important factor in the process from animate being to personal being via a theory of self is what Harré calls 'supplementation,' as when the mother makes up what is still defective in a child's personhood. True personal being and moral status is achieved when the symbiotic relationship is 'dissolved to some notable extent' and supplementations are no longer needed. Harré concludes. 'I have argued that what makes a being a person is the possession and use of a certain theory [of the self] in terms of which that being constructs and orders its beliefs, plans, feelings and actions.'[19] Jansz puts it more succinctly: 'The person is the source model of the self.'[20]

The contingency of personal being is underlined when Harré acknowledges that 'there may be societies whose members can never achieve personal being because the practice of individual transformation of social resources does not exist.'[21] Interestingly however, as we have seen, he concedes that the 'centred' model of experience is not a dispensable option in our psychology or moral order.[22] It is a permanent feature providing a perennial temptation to believe in an extra being, a noumenal self deeply embedded within our persons. The self, modelling itself on the person which is publicly locatable, looks for a psychologically locatable substantial centre, the inner me. But this is an illusion (though a necessary one), because the self is in fact only an imparted organizing theory. It seems that if the self, like God, does not exist, it is necessary to invent it! – at least in our society.

Pluralism and Personhood

In anticipation, one might point here to parallels and contrasts between Harré's anthropological pluralism and John Hick's theological pluralism. Hick adopts a constructionist approach but still retains a noumenal though utterly mysterious God, or rather 'Reality.'[23] Were Harré to address theological rather than psychological questions, he might argue that a centred model of the universe is indeed indispensable in our universe, but against Hick he would presumably insist that the temptation to believe in an extra being, a noumenal God or Reality deeply embedded within it, must be resisted. Thus, he might echo Don Cupitt's assertion that 'God is the central unifying symbol of the religious life,' and agree with Cupitt's more recent comment that 'we have no reason to speak of a metaphysical soul on this side of the flux of language-formed events, or of any metaphysical Reality out there on the far side of language-formed events.'[24] Yet according to these arguments, it might seem that it is only by believing in an inner active core of the universe, and of ourselves, that our spiritual attributes and our spiritual as well as moral order can be realized – God and the inner self stand or fall together. If so, the loss of the inner active core of the self, or of the universe, can be expected to lead to the collapse of our moral and spiritual order – and this seems to be happening today. It might seem a little odd that the realization and integration of the cosmic and moral order should rest on an unreality – a temptation to be avoided!

I will be arguing that a Constructionist approach has both challenging and illuminating implications for Christian understanding, but that it need not lead to either Harré's or Hick's conclusions; it need not rule out the reality of selfhood or of God; nor must it entail a radically pluralist anthropology or theology. First it is necessary to pursue further how different theories of the self may be generated in animate beings.

Harré describes how traditional Eskimos, Japanese, and Amerindians of Yucatan have very different concepts of selfhood, which are reflected in their languages, their pronouns (or lack of them) and differing forms of address.[25] Eskimo languages, variants of Inuit, lack self-reflexive terms it seems, e.g. 'myself', and the Eskimo accordingly can scarcely experience himself or herself, apart from family and community. Individual morality is virtually nonsense. The Japanese have more subtly complex relationships but, again, it seems that, traditionally at least, they could hardly think of themselves except in relation to others, rather than in relation to their own thoughts and feelings. (It would appear that one could speak of a good husband or wife, soldier, athlete, or politician, but not of a good person). These examples are offered as evidence that a sense of selfhood is not universal, or innate, but specific and given, by parents, culture, society and religion.[26]

Harré admits that 'the idea that linguistic forms determine psychological structures is far too simplistic,' but he can still write 'The general principle of this work' is that there is 'nothing in the mind that was not first in conversation,'[27] which, for Harré, includes the theory of the self, without which there is no self.

One can agree that personal relationships are essential for a baby to grow into a person, yet against the view outlined above it might be argued that, not only is the potential to become a person innate and present in the very structure of the infant's brain, as Harré would agree, but that, the actualization of this potential is the 'proper' fulfilment, even if not always realized, of all human beings. Such fulfilment can be realized in a manner unique to the particularity of every human being, yet also conforming to the shared character of *human* being. Further, one might suggest that this fulfilment embraces not only the cognitive, but the emotional potential of human beings. Harré almost admits to this when he mentions recent discoveries in developmental psychology which have shown us reciprocal influences between members of a symbiotic dyad. The behaviour of infants calls forth a certain specific subrange of the possible repertoire of speech acts available to the mother, ensuring the suitability of her supplementations.[28]

Yet the only example he gives of what the infant calls for is a food source! There is, however, much evidence to indicate that infants actively seek not only food, but an emotional relationship with their primary care givers from birth (before conversation has begun to fill their minds), and that they are not as passive as Harré tends to suggest, but are active participants in the relationship. Murray and Stein write that 'it seems to be the case that the human infant is predisposed to respond to human qualities as special categories of experience,'[29] while Jansz notes that 'the child appears as an active contribuant [*sic*] to the development of internalization.'[30] One might simply say that what infants seek to call forth, even if wordlessly, is love. It is not only animate but yearning, yearning to love and be loved. What it needs perhaps is not merely a theory of self as organizer of itself and its world, but a theory of self as loving and loveable, and perhaps more than just a theory of itself, a discovery of what it is and can be.

If we turn to resources in the Christian tradition, we might think here with Irenaeus, of the human being intended by God to grow into his image and likeness (*Adv. Haeres.* V.xvi.1),[31] or as we might say, endowed with the potential for true personhood, indeed yearning for this goal, but frustrated. Why? Irenaeus would say it was because the first human beings were seduced by the devil (IV.xl.3). We might say it was and is because human beings are seduced by false or inadequate theories of selfhood or by insufficient supplementations. What is sought and what is given is not the same. What is provided in practice in human social relationships is not ideal, not the perfect likeness of God, not the adequate 'answer' to human yearning, but something falling short, perhaps very far short of that potential ideal. With or without Irenaeus, the point here would be that the infant may seek, but what it is given in relationships can profoundly affect what it becomes, and what it may become may be far from healthy.

Despite these qualifications, we may yet look to the Constructionist account to shed light on what it means to be, or become a person, and recognize some important implications.

1. If persons are engendered by different theories of self in different social systems, the degree and depth of diversity is likely to be much greater than is usually supposed. Mutual understanding between members of different cultures (or sexes) is therefore likely to be far harder to achieve than we often assume, though not necessarily impossible.

2. The problems of mutual understanding would arise not only between different cultures, but within them where conditions varied. What theory of self or sense of personhood has been/is being given in depressed refugee camps, in impoverished inner cities or shanty towns? or for that matter in homes and families where value is conceived of only in terms of cash value or usefulness to consumerist society? Further, what right has a person in a different setting shaped by a different theory of self to condemn those who have not been given the gift of personhood? How can someone who has never been given a sense of the reality and value and responsibility of being a person, be expected to recognize the value of other persons? Maybe we are not as morally justified as we like to think in condemning the vandal, the kidnapper, the terrorist, or a Saddam Hussein. Yet if we do presume to call them to a better way of personhood, must we not assume that there is something there, common to all human beings, not merely a theory, but some latent potential able to respond?

3. On the more positive side, it might be argued that we should be more ready to search out and delight in the rich varieties of personal being in the world around us, not assuming that what is different must be inferior, but ready to share what is ours and open to new possibilities .

But just as in the case of religious pluralism, so also with anthropological pluralism, the question of discrimination arises. Social scientists like Harré

Chapter 1

may simply point to the differences in the world, to the Japanese and the Eskimos, not to mention the Amerindians of Yucatan, as evidence of the rich variety of life and leave it at that. Yet even he arrives at the conclusion that 'to be a *social* being is not a moral status', while '*personal* being is a moral status in itself.'[32] Similarly Jansz maintains that 'person and morality are inextricably linked, the *person* is a moral category, because personhood is implied in a 'moral world' of how things (including persons) ought to be.'[33] Indeed, on the grounds that intentionality and autonomy are at the core of any person-concept, Harré can say that 'value accrues to human beings just in so far as they are seen to be intentional actors because by that alone they can lay claim to personhood, to a place in the moral order.'[34] Apart from the problem he poses over the value of the disabled, this conclusion comes close to claiming superiority for particular theories of self, as against simply acknowledging the rich variety of life. However, some of the variety is not rich, as already indicated; it is often tragically impoverished, and destructive.

We cannot escape value judgements, and Christians are those people who set the highest value on the person because they begin with the person of Jesus, or his way of being a person in the world, which they believe is nothing less than the true way, God's way. If this is not to be an arbitrary and arrogant assumption, it will be necessary to suggest how this could be so in terms of human self-understanding, for all its diversity. It is here that the views of developmental psychologists are relevant. It may be that the project of becoming a person in the way of Jesus is right not just for some but for all human beings, not just because we call this God's way, but because this way lies the true and ultimate fulfilment of the primal groping and yearning of the human infant, and not just of the infant, but of all human beings in their continuing search. for personhood, a search which need not, and perhaps should not end, while temporal life endures.[35]

We turn then to the person of Jesus to explore first some of the implications of the Constructionist account of person-making in relation to him, and then to see how his story might bear on the Social Constructionist account of personal being. It would seem that in the process of Jesus' becoming truly a person, far more significance should attach to what he was given in personal relationships after rather than before his birth. What the implications of this may be for the doctrine of Virginal conception I will leave aside, but it would appear that the response to his initial search for emotional relationship would have been of fundamental importance.

Thus one might suppose that his mother and father, like other Mums and Dads, had a crucial role to play as person-makers. If 'what makes a human being a person is possession and use of a certain theory' (cf. n. 13), one might ponder how dependent he was not only on his parents, but on their society and its history, which on the Social Constructionist view becomes profoundly relevant to the forging of his personhood. However, this need in no way detract from the uniqueness of personhood which became actualized in him. This, made actual and visible in Jesus' life story, could then constitute a theory of selfhood now made publicly and socially available. As such it was available not only to be imparted to animate beings from scratch, so to speak, but also to reconstitute persons already shaped or being shaped by alternative and perhaps inadequate theories of self. Jansz hints all too tentatively at this when he writes that 'an individual expression of selfhood, originating in a person's self-narrative, may sometimes be taken up by a community and thus give way to a 'new' element in a convention of personhood.'[36] Is this where we might locate the experience of being born again and the creation of the Church?[37]

Certainly the appearance in history of actualized true personal being, were it to happen, would constitute a challenge to those persons more or less defectively shaped by defective theories; at the same time it would constitute a call to embark upon a new way of being a person. The response to what was externally offered might be spoken of as obedience to the call, but it would not be 'heteronomous' (i.e. imposed from outside) if what was offered externally, in fact corresponded to the inner reality, the true potential for personal being of the one responding. Rather, obedient service would be perfect freedom. In so far as the call to personal being was to being in relationship, personal beings thus actualized or being actualized in their responding would, or should, constitute a challenge and call to others to respond to their potential for personal being in relationship.

Here one might indeed locate the Church and its task in continuing to actualize and mediate in every time and place, the reality on which it was founded at a particular time, in a particular place. To return to that foundation, whatever the role of Jesus' home and parents, there must also have come a time for him, as for any human infant, when the reality of being a person was not only something he was given, but something he could work for. As Harré writes, '... under certain conditions one's own personal being can become one's own project... As psychological symbiosis dissolves, we take over the work of the dominant dyad within which we were created.'[38] In other words, his mother's supplementations yield to his own self-mastery.

Chapter 1

However, this is not the automatic outcome for human beings. Harré goes on to argue that 'a necessary condition for personhood as we conceive it' is for 'the locus of control' to shift to 'the junior member within a symbiotic dyad.'[39] In short, Mums or Dads must let their child grow up. Yet not only parents may obstruct this. 'There are societies in which personal mental life is immoral, and the person theory at least officially admits personal reference only within some form of psychological symbiosis.' Alternatively, there may be those people who are unwilling or unable to grow up, 'some animate beings are persons only when they are in psychological symbiosis with a partner, who is willing and ready to do the person work for them. One's personhood may be displayed not through one's own efforts, but by the supplementation of one's own defective display by the senior partner of the dyad.'[40]

Yet the dissolution of psychological symbiosis is necessary for the moral ideal to be achieved; 'whoever strives to achieve personal being must seek both honour and autonomy.'[41] One might wish to qualify this hint of Pelagianism,[42] by suggesting that honour and autonomy need not only to be sought, but to be given, if they are to be realized. One might see this process dramatically illustrated in the story of Jesus' disciples living in dependency on him, until they discovered their autonomy in the moment that he let himself be taken from them.[43] However, the term 'autonomy' must be used with care, not as signifying self-centred individualism and total self-reliance, but in terms of achieving the degree of centredness and freedom necessary for entering into personal relationships, and for love and responsibility to be possible. To continue with Harré, in the 'ultimate degree, when action is unconditioned by any rule whatever, the greater the moral worth of the actor.'[44] One might qualify this in terms of being unconditioned by – or free from – any external rule that does not correspond to the 'Law' of one's own being. It is hard to deny that value judgements are involved here, but perhaps it would be wrong to pretend otherwise simply for fear of giving offence.

Space precludes going into great detail, but Christians would certainly recognize in the Constructionist account much of what they would want to say about the person of Jesus, and his moral freedom and authority. Perhaps that is no accident, as the theory under discussion is one powerfully shaped by the theory of selfhood derived from Jesus.

However, Harré's account may still not go far enough. In the quotation above, moral worth seems to depend on the elimination of supplementations leading to a complete autonomy in stark loneliness, no longer dependent on personal relationships. A distinction needs to be drawn between supplementations characteristic of dependent relationships, which are necessary aids towards maturing as persons, and should diminish in time else they will obstruct that process, and those supplementations by which persons sustain each other in mutual mature relationships, in giving and receiving in the way that lies at the heart of love. To deny any need of supplementation in the former sense, to claim complete self-reliance, would be tantamount to a refusal to recognize our finitude – the incompleteness of our personhood at every stage in life. To deny any need or room for supplementation in the latter sense (as essential to human mutuality), would be a denial of personal being as being-in-relationship – as actualized in total giving and receiving in love.[45]

So Harré may be right as far as he goes in arguing that true moral status is achieved when psychological dependency yields to moral autonomy (at least to a high degree). However, this should be seen not as the goal of personal being, but its take-off point, as the point at which it becomes possible to give oneself for the sake of others. This is the moment when persons achieve the freedom to give themselves to enable others to become persons. In other words, the achievement of personal being is the moment when love – true, unselfish, un-selfcentred love can be actualized, when creation and salvation coincide (to adapt Tillich's dictum).[46] Without a self one cannot give oneself. What is given, one might suppose, is more than a theory.

The Biblical records testify to Jesus as a person who somehow was able to transcend the theories of self available in his social situation. He actualized a way of personal being that startled his contemporaries, and seemed threatening to social groups shaped by and still shaping different ideas of selfhood. Jesus spoke and acted with authority; not out of self-interest (if the evidence can be trusted at all), but in the interest of other selves, those lacking honour, self-esteem or social value, or till then the capacity to achieve fully personal being and moral status.

For Jesus to become the person he was – to stand within and yet beyond the theories of selfhood of his day, and to be able to open up new possibilities for others, he would not only have had to internalize and employ the theory bestowed on him in his infancy; he must also have been willing to loosen its hold, to let it go in response to new possibilities of personal being. This may be seen in the story of Jesus' encounter with the unexpected faith of the Roman centurion; he 'heard him with astonishment' (Matthew 8:10), an astonishment that illustrates an openness to others that

Chapter 1

involved letting go of past theories. One might dare to suggest that this could happen not only in interaction with other persons, but in interaction with that which is the source of all being – God. If so, Jesus' openness to personal being would pertain not only to his relationships with other persons, but with God. In the terms argued above, this would reflect his awareness of his finitude (as against self-idolatry) in his humanity, and his need of supplementation. It would belong to and grow out of his life of prayer, as, we may suppose, it should also for anyone else.

However it happened, what the New Testament portrays is Jesus as person who could make other persons, who could confer the gift of personhood on often the most unpromising material. He was person-maker par excellence. Yet we may accept that the power of person-making in him was in the first place the same in principle as in any Mum or Dad, the power of love, Love makes persons, and enables them in turn to become person-makers. However, what social constructionsts may help us to see is that love is not enough. Love could be expressed by concentration camp guards towards their children. Accompanied by their deformed theory of self, it could help to create monsters like themselves. To overcome such deformities, love must be accompanied by a theory of self capable of opening the way to the achievement of true personal being. This must involve the identification of and rejection of defective or inadequate theories of self – in short, judgement, and indeed condemnation, not of persons but of inadequate theories, not to destroy, but to create new beginnings on the path towards achieving true personhood.

Nazism is not of course alone in offering a defective theory of self, though it manifested and actualized the worst possibilities. For all our fears of Christian arrogance, it remains the case that in the light of Christ, it is at least coherent to recognize theories of self that give rise to different kinds of persons, who to a greater or lesser extent accord with the personhood of Christ. To challenge the adequacy of Nazism or Communism, individualism or collectivism, consumerism or any other socially imposed understanding of human being, need not spring from pride in oneself, least of all when the criterion of selfhood is not one's own achievement, but recognized as something given and unearned; nor need it imply unqualified criticism – far from it. To see true personal being in Christ, is to be able to recognize pathways towards it, often far outside the Christian tradition, and also to see pathways within the Christian tradition all too often blocked and choked. Either way, recourse to the story of Jesus may keep the pathways open. To look the other way, to refrain from questioning any apparently blocked route or unhealthy theory, could be judged to be as irresponsible as refusing to question a wrong diagnosis of disease. Would anyone who found a cure for AIDS not wish to publish it? How much more serious it is, if not just bodily but spiritual health is at stake – the question of truly human personal being.

In the West the inadequacy of Descartes' 'I think, therefore I am' has become increasingly apparent. He may have proved he was an individual, or a thinking machine, but not a person. To be a person is more to be able to say, with Augustine, 'I am loved, therefore I am'. I am in relationship, and therefore a person, or at least on the way to true personal being. However, here in the world we have many different relationships. Does that mean we are multi-persons? The answer to that is a partial 'yes'. In a way, like the Japanese, we are all different persons to different people. The way we speak on the telephone often gives the game away. The crucial question is, whether beneath our various public persons there is an underlying reality which is more than a mere theory. Or putting it differently, is an underlying (transcendent) reality coming into being, on the enabling basis of a theory of self, but not reducible to it any more than the mind is reducible without remainder to the brain (despite what reductionists may argue)? Harré may be right to say that no substantial self, no 'inner me' is to be found on the biological or even psychological plane of human being, but wrong to suppose that something real is not coming into being on a different plane, the spiritual, which is not subject to the methodology of biology or psychology.[47] A perennial temptation for natural and social scientists has been to suppose that nothing can be real which is not accessible to their particular methodology. In the light of what he says about the Japanese, Harré argues that there are different selves in different relationships. On the supposition that the self is only a theory and not a substantial entity, he questions whether one can really attribute continuity of selfhood to anyone. The continuity is only in the publicly locatable person employing the theory, and if the theory incorporated is weak in self-reference or incorporates diversification or fragmentation or simply breaks down, we can expect a loss of continuity of personhood. This may help to explain the confused condition of multiple personality with which we began.

As a matter of empirical sociological observation, a lack of integrated selfhood may be a fact, yet still an impoverishment, leading to a fragmentation of human personhood, which imposes a limitation on human relationships and an obstacle to the achievement of personal being. At one extreme this may shed light on those Nazis who really did apparently love their wives and children and want the best for them, and yet would treat other human beings barbarically.[48] Far removed from them in every way, there may be people like the Eskimos with apparently very little sense of differentiated selfhood at all. On Harré's own account this state falls short of true personal being. We may agree, and without any wish to be judgemental, see this condition as in some measure impoverished. In a very harsh environment it may have provided a successful strategy for survival; more than that, it may testify to possibilities, often not realized elsewhere, of communal mutual support. Yet the non-realization of the human potentiality for personal being and moral responsibility, and the consequent limitation on human relationships, may be regarded as a loss.

We might say, then, that personal being emerges not only on the basis of a theory of self, but through differentiation and integration in personal relationship. Differentiation is a constant condition of becoming and being a person. It occurs in relationships with the other, many others, as we discover ourselves as persons in relation to other persons. As Jansz observes, 'persons in conversation are actively constructing each others' 'selves', as well as their own 'self' in joint action.'[49] The integration of personhood – the integration of our various self theories or various uncoordinated aspects of some underlying theory of self, is, I suggest, harder to achieve than the differentiation. Relationships with different people in different contexts are socially inevitable. But the capacity for self-integration is not socially or psychologically inevitable. Yet without this capacity, discontinuity of personhood is likely to result, as appears to be the case in traditional Japanese society. Alternatively, the self theory with which we were originally endowed may prove inadequate to cope with new experiences and new relationships, and so when threatened, lead to fanatical and destructive self-defence, or collapse into disconnected parts.

Reintegration of personhood might then seem to depend not on a static theory of self, but on the continuing revision or reconstruction of the given theory, if it is to embrace and facilitate the ordering of new experiences of relationship with other persons. In other words, 'the self' may indeed be a theory, and not the real thing; but what is it that employs the theory, and comes into being through it, and lets it be changed again and again for a more adequate theory? Something must transcend any given theory of self if what is new is to be embraced. Without that possibility we would seem bound to cling to what has been given by past social formations and to force what is new to fit what is already given (even then the occurrence of the 'given' remains inexplicable). This would seem to be the way of alienation and idolatry.[50] Alternatively we might postulate a self-transcending reality and call it 'spirit'[51] – something inchoate, or no more than potential at birth in what looks like a merely animate being, but which comes into being or into fuller being in the process of self-discovery, a process lasting through life in response to and within ever new personal relationships and experiences, however 'astonishing'.

We might then wonder how the self-transcending self or spirit can reintegrate itself without, as it were, a platform to stand upon. Yet perhaps it does have such a platform – a personal relationship which transcends and embraces all personal relationships, in terms of or in relation to which (or whom) the integration of personal being with all personal beings becomes possible; in short, in relation to God. It might then be said that the true frame of reference for persons is not just 'society', but 'society as other personal beings in relation to a personal God'.[52]

In these terms, personal being is not something we possess, which sociologists can observe *in toto*, but something we can achieve, not as isolated individuals but in constant relationship with the ultimately personal, loving and all-embracing God, who transcends our selves (or self-theories), enabling what is new to enlarge and perhaps correct what is already there, and through whom our relationships with others are integrated. Thus in relationship with God, our relationships with others need not lead to fragmentation or result in defensive exclusiveness, but can give rise to a diversification which enlarges and enriches our own personhood through the widening process of differentiation. At the same time this widening differentiation is drawn into a fuller and deeper integration. Here again we may see the vital importance of prayer (understood as openness to God) for the process of reintegrating our differentiated personhood into wholeness.

Such reintegration is not to be conceived of individualistically as the goal to be reached outside relationship, as if relationships were merely a means to an end. It is rather the precondition of true relationship, of being an 'I' in relation to a 'thou', without being cut off from or submerged in the other. The wholeness of personhood therefore has no place apart from relationship, apart from the self-transcending wholeness of community or *koinonia*, anchored in the transcendent God, who holds differentiated selves in personal wholeness and differentiated persons in a larger wholeness, which is or should be the Church and ultimately the kingdom of God.

Returning to Harré, we can agree that personhood is **gift** before

Chapter 1

achievement; it is the gift from persons to those not yet persons, which meets their deepest yearnings though by no means always their conscious desires. It is a gift that confers otherness without isolation, differentiation without separation – the two conditions apart from which personal relationships would be impossible. The gift makes possible but cannot compel the personal response which creates personal relationship, and without which personhood remains only an idea, a potentiality, not a reality.

Much of this could be said of the spontaneous, unselfconscious life of families, of Mums and Dads, as they make possible and then delight in the response of their children as growing persons. At least it could be said of many, but sadly not of all families. This shows once again that being or becoming a person is not natural in the sense of an innate, automatic condition; it is a project to be undertaken, freely and consciously, and which depends on others, on family, on community, and ultimately on God.

A project implies a goal. It is when we recognize the limitations of Mums and Dads and other human persons that we may come to realize that, left to ourselves, we cannot reach the goal of full personhood. What other persons offer us falls short of our yearning. Our hearts are restless till they find their rest in true personal being. More prosaically, personhood cannot be realized until given by and in our responding to the ultimately personal, the personal God whom Christians believe they meet in Jesus, who was himself somehow the potential of personhood and person-making power become actual. This is one way, if not the only way, of understanding the mystery of the Incarnation. The actualization of personal being in Jesus does not rule out the possibility of direct encounter with God, however that may be understood, but it proves that such a special experience is no longer essential for the realization of personhood. The way to this goal was opened up for Jesus' disciples in and through the human historical life of Jesus, and through his disciples in every generation the way can be opened to others, so long as those disciples do not point to themselves, but to the source of their personal being.

One might propose here a variant of the cosmological argument. The old argument postulated a self-existent Creator to explain creation. Instead we postulate the reality of the Ultimately Personal to explain persons or the coming-to-be of persons, and more particularly to account for the appearance in a world of incomplete, imperfect persons of one true person, called Jesus. One would have to be careful here not to portray Jesus as the 'perfect person' in static terms. Rather we may see in him a dynamic growing into personhood which nothing in this world could impede, which was real and actual, which achieved 'honour and autonomy', which led finally to and indeed made possible an act of total self-giving unconditioned by any rule whatever, when he accepted rejection and death at the hands of the rule-makers. In this sense Jesus is the proof of the existence of God; his coming to be as person is evidence for the transcendent power of person-making. For humanity he is the giver and the gift, the socially locatable source of a dynamic (not fixed or static) theory of self, which was actualized in his own being, and hence became available to others. Jansz writes with customary reserve that whatever resources a person has 'borrowed' from the public collective domain and constructed into his private individual self-narrative, he may return with 'a little interest'.[53] In Jesus' case we might prefer to speak of a massive dividend!

The book which witnesses to Jesus cannot on its own be enough: a book cannot give itself as a person can, and to tie the personal God too closely to any book is to risk unpersonalising him, which is fatal, and in the case of the Bible, inexcusable.[54] To treat anything penultimate, even the Bible, as ultimate is to render it demonic. Obedience to a book in its objective externality cannot of itself be obedience to the call of true personal being; the call which comes from without but which finds its authentification within in the coming-to-be of personhood. If this is the 'God within' it is not without remainder, because one's own being is embraced in that which embraces all personal beings.

The New Testament explicitly presents itself as witness to God not enbooked but enpersoned in Jesus, and in him inaugurating a new living personal relationship that transcends the moment of Jesus' lifetime and embraces or offers to embrace all lifetimes in living relationship. Thus we think of the human spirit coming into being in a process of continuous creation – God's work of creation did not end after six days! However, this coming-into-being depends on openness to the divine Spirit – God, in living relationship. For Christians the symbol 'Father' signifies God as the source of all life. If the gender connotations offend, then other images must be found, but it is the same God who is the source of personal life who is made visible and actual in the person of Jesus. Through him the power of becoming persons reaches us when the human spirit is drawn into enlivening relationship with the Holy Spirit. The Trinity thus becomes the symbol of the living God, the creator of persons, male and female, drawing them into being out of the matrix of psychological, sociological, and animate life, itself emerging from the physical cosmic

Chapter 1

structure reaching back to the Big Bang and the impenetrable mystery of its source.

However, if that is what the Holy Trinity is, the living relationship into which to live and grow as persons, we cannot afford to shove it aside ('it', indeed!) like a metaphysical Rubik's cube that cannot be solved and would get you nowhere if it could be. Cut off from God in the Trinity, our very existence as persons is at risk. Precisely because personhood is not automatic, but gift and achievement, the loss of personhood, the denial of personhood, is a real possibility. Such loss is not just theoretically regrettable, but potentially disastrous. In other words, the glorious goal of becoming persons in relationship (call it heaven), is matched by the terrible prospect of the loss or non-realization of personal being' (call it hell), but it may not be in a different world from ours. The media provides evidence enough of the hellish consequences of not treating or valuing human beings as persons, as when they are reduced to the level of objects, treated as things, crushed, broken, fragmented. Or, if not completely crushed, they retaliate out of their depersonalized experience to destroy others in furious vengeance. They are quite unable to restore themselves as persons, because that is 'gift before achievement'; if it has not been – is not being – given, how can it be achieved? They can only begin to become persons when they are accepted as persons, respected as persons, loved as persons, and shown what it means, in other words, when they are not only presented with an adequate theory of selfhood, but embraced by a community of persons within which to grow.

That may not be as simple as one would like to think – there is a price to pay. Those who for any reason have inherited or acquired a defective or inadequate theory of self have nevertheless been shaped by it. To be treated as persons in a way that contradicts their own self-perception may pose a fundamental threat to their identity. Its surrender may seem to entail too great a risk of total self loss. The making or remaking of persons would thus seem to call for person-breaking, as well as person-making power. For the breaking and making to be effected on the 'inside' from the 'outside,' without personal moral autonomy being lost in the process, would be a remarkable happening. The possibility might be discerned in an act of total self-giving for the sake of other selves, which once recognized, could be seen not as a threat to be resisted, but as a gift to be received, a call to be responded to, indeed a new liberating, creative opportunity to be grasped.

The mystery of how it could come about, of how the apparent breaking of one person could open the path for the unlimited making or remaking of persons is one we cannot pursue further here. However, the complete acceptance of the unpersoned and the marginalized at the risk and fact of torture and death, would certainly reveal person-making power at work at the heart of human destructiveness. What we know is that when that was seen in the life and death of Jesus of Nazareth, a new power of person-making of an unprecedented kind was launched into the world, generated we could say by the combination of person-affirming love and a radically new theory of selfhood. Once received, it offered liberation from soul-destroying constraints and a foundation for a new way of personal being in the world.

Those to whom this gift of personhood has been and is being conferred can scarcely refrain, without self-contradiction, from wishing to share it with others. If the yearning of the human spirit for the realization of personal being – being in relationship – is brought about by an act of total self-giving for others, how can the process help but replicate itself in the sacrificial sharing of the gift? In so far as persons cannot find fulfilment in isolation, their task cannot be less than to pass on the gift they have received. This must mean carrying on the work of helping to create persons out of human beings, to do so within relationship and in so doing to enlarge and enrich the relationships within which they themselves grow as persons.

There is more than politics involved here, but pursuit of this task cannot help but involve politics. It is the inescapable task of persons to help make persons, by responding to others as persons, at any age, not just to animate beings at birth, and it is the duty of person-builders to resist every force, every theory, every policy, right-wing or left-wing, and every form of religion, not least within Christianity, that depersonalizes members of society and treats persons as things or categories or classes or as anything less than persons.

My conclusion, then, is that becoming a person is the true goal of human life, at least on earth. The possibilities of personhood are infinitely varied, and so are the aberrations. There is certainly more to it than self-creation, which in fact can only be self-defeating. Individualism, oneself isolated from others, is as tragic an aberration as communism, the self lost in the collective. Individual self-fulfilment may sound hypothetically possible but is a spiritual disaster, because the fundamental yearning of human beings is to be persons, to become real in relationship. Personal fulfilment is therefore impossible without the others, or outside the embrace of the transcendent power of personal being.

Chapter 1

Finally, we return to the question of a correlation between the idea that God is merely a human construct, and that the sense of personhood is merely a human construct. To suppose that both are nothing but human constructs is to lose any basis for discrimination between one view of God and another, and equally between one way of viewing and being human and any other. This point of view is intelligible but disastrous; it undermines the very concept of humanity. Polytheism and polyanthropism go hand in hand, as do atheism and 'ananthropism' (the rejection not only of God but of common humanity). None of these alternatives can satisfy the universal human quest for true being as persons – the longed-for state in which fragmented, stunted or distorted selfhoods are healed and fulfilled.

This raises the question of the place of religions as the bearers, not only of concepts of God but of theories of self. The two issues are so closely related that it is no accident that where the reality of a personal God is denied, the reality of personal being is likely to be denied, as in Buddhism, whereas where a personal God is affirmed, as in the Judaeo-Christian tradition and Islam, personal being is likely to be affirmed. However, in practice there is clearly much in Buddhism, especially in Mahayana Buddhism, that is congruous with the actualization of personal being, and much in Jewish, Christian, and Islamic history that has and still does militate against it. Employing Harré's analysis but not necessarily sharing his conclusions, we might say that wherever defective theories of self (generating defective forms of personal being) are discerned, they need to be challenged. The defect may be incompleteness, or more seriously, premature foreclosing – treating as ultimate what is less than ultimate, and so rendering what may be good in itself, demonic. If defective self-theories need correction (redemption), so must defective God or 'Reality' theories. On the other hand, what may be conducive to personal being can be affirmed, whatever its provenance. It is here that we may locate pluralism. The richness of diversity can be fully affirmed in its penultimacy, but if it is held to be ultimate, if differentiation alone claims to be all, the outcome is, as we have seen, fragmentation and spiritual apartheid – a threat to our common humanity. Without the transcendent power of integration – an integration that does not overwhelm diversity but embraces it – not only the identity of human beings, but of the human community falls apart. The multiple personality of fragmented humankind desperately needs healing, above all in the face of the resurgence of demonic nationalism or racism.

In conclusion, I have examined Social Constructionism and explored its often illuminating insights into the nature of personal being in general, and its implications for understanding the personal being of Jesus in particular. At the same time, drawing on Biblical testimony to the personal being of Jesus, I have contested some of the conclusions drawn by Social Constructionists such as Harré and Jansz. In short, I have argued in defence of two propositions which not all may share, but which are of considerable significance: first, that there is something common to all human beings, which goes far beyond the state of merely animate being in which they first appear on earth. That something extra is the potential in human beings for personal being and for the coming-to-be of the human spirit. This serves to legitimate the concept of common humanity not merely as a biological fact but as a moral obligation, not just for some cultures and communities, but for all. Secondly, I have argued that the power of person-making and the criterion of every person-making project (that is, every religion and ideology), is found in Jesus of Nazareth. Such a statement of faith may be bound to offend those who are searching for their true selves outside the frame of Christianity, but some idea of a common goal seems to me to be a condition of a common humanity, such that in all its rich variety it can matter to me, and not have to be regarded as an exotic curiosity or disregarded as none of my business because it does not rest on my theory of selfhood.

If not Jesus, then someone or something else must be ultimately true for us all, or we do not belong together and have no moral obligation to each other. However, what is the worth of a moral order from which any fellow human being is ultimately excluded? If something or someone else, not Jesus, is claimed to have the key, then their claims need to be tested. If Jesus holds the key, then no one has grounds for boasting or arrogance, because what comes through him is gift before it is achievement, and is never achievement without others or the working of the divine Spirit. If he is the true personal being for all, then I am my brothers' and sisters' keeper. We are united in a common humanity within which there is room for the rich diversity of human personality, but also for distortions and perversions that may lead to a cross.

The next task is to explore how Jesus, despite his apparently crushing defeat on the cross, came to be acknowledged as ultimate (as Lord). In particular, I will try to show how the language and imagery of sacrifice could be enriched sufficiently to express this conviction.

Chapter 1

Notes

1 This chapter was originally published in *The World of Religions: Essays on historical and contemporary issues*, eds. G.W. Trompf and G. Hamel (Dehli, 2002). It is published here with the kind permission of the editors.

2 *The Guardian* (London) 9 November 1990.

3 Cf. Mk. 5:9 on the healing of 'Legion'.

4 Ludwig Feuerbach, German nineteenth-century philosopher who pioneered the idea that God is nothing other than a human projection.

5 Especially Harré 1984 and Jansz 1991.

6 McFadyen 1990. For another theological discussion of personhood, see Schwöbel and Gunton (eds.) 1991; and for an extensive historical survey of the matter at hand, see Taylor 1989.

7 Harré 1984, 108 (emphasis original); cf. 161.

8 Ibid., 77.

9 Ibid., 144.

10 Jansz 1991, 117 ff.

11 In Harré (ed.) 1976, 40.

12 Jansz 1991, 125.

13 Harré 1984, 104.

14 Harré in Peacock and Gillett (eds.) 1976, 100 ff. Cf. McFadyen 1990, 93: 'I shall be arguing that there is no substantial personal core, but that personal centring is enabled by holding a belief or theory about oneself without which personal life in the network of responsibilities which constitute a morally structured world would be impossible.' (No explicit reference to Harré is given here, though a considerable debt is acknowledged elsewhere.)

15 Harré 1984, 76 (first two quotations), 93, 167 (others), cf. pp. 161, 214.

16 Jansz 1991, 2.

17 Harré 1984, 93, 106.

18 Ibid 1984, 107.

19 Ibid 1984, 104, 214, 248, 270.

20 Jansz 1991, 55; cf. 129.

21 Harré 1984, 23.

22 See *supra*, n. 5. Cf. McFadyen 1991, 98: 'The self... is not a substance but a means of organizing one's experience, thought, knowledge, beliefs, action, etc. as *though* centred on a substantial inner core' (emphasis original). He goes on to discuss the 'deep self' in relation to 'local selves' in a manner reminiscent of John Hick's discussion of myths or metaphors in relation to Reality. Cf. p. 102: 'Deep "self" would then be a transcendent point of unity behind a number of lower level models.'

23 Hick 1989, 240 ff.

24 Earlier Cupitt, 1980, 94 derives his non-realist view of God not from Feuerbach but from Kant's *Critique of Pure Reason* (1771); cf. Cupitt 1994, 17.

25 Peacock and Gillett (eds.) 1976, 106 ff.

26 For the example of the Maori, see Harré 1984, 89 ff., and for numerous others and a useful bibliography, see Jansz 1991, 66 ff. The latter writes: 'In the Gahuku-Gama conception of the person there is 'no essential separation of the individual from the social pattern; social roles and social status are not distinguished from the individuals who enact them' (quoting K.E. Read, 'Morality and the concept of the Person among the Gahuku-Gama,' *Oceania* 25 [1955], 233–82).

27 Harré 1984, 116.

28 Ibid., 250.

29 Murray and Stein in Woodhead, Carr and Light (eds.) 1991, 149 ff.

30 Op. cit. 133.

31 It is God who 'from the beginning even to the end, forms us and prepares us for life, and is present with his handiwork, and perfects it after the image and likeness of God.' See also IV, xxviii ff. for the theme of humanity not created perfect but intended to grow in relationship to God.

32 Harré 1984, 270 (my emphasis).

33 Jansz 1991, 64.

34 Harré 1984, 272.

35 McFadyen (1990, 8) has no qualms about advocating a normative account of personhood against many possible distortions. It is no accident that he assumes from the start a normative (Christian) account of God. (cf. 1, 45 ff.).

36 Jansz 1991, 141.

37 Cf. Jansz 1991, 118, n. 4.

38 Harré 1984, 258. He adds, 'and that includes people-making work'.

39 Ibid, 266.

40 Ibid 1984, 266 (first quotation), 270 (second).

41 Ibid 1984, 270.

42 Pelagius was the first world-class British heretic, who, in the early fifth century, was somewhat unfairly condemned for teaching that salvation depended on personal effort without the necessity of grace. See Kelly 1977, 357.

43 Cf. John 16:7: 'Nevertheless I tell you the truth: it is for your own good that I am leaving you' – words written almost certainly with *retrospective* insight in the aftermath of Jesus' death.

44 Harré 1984, 262.

45 It might be interesting to explore this distinction in relation to Jesus' historical life and his place in the eternal triune life of God, but space forbids.

46 Tillich 1978, ii, 44, where he argues that in a sense 'Creation and Fall coincide'.

47 McFadyen employs the suggestive metaphor of 'sedimentation' for the process of acquiring a uniquely centred personal identity. The danger with this and the associated concept of the 'deep "self"' transcending 'the immediacy of particular relations' (or 'local selves') is that of implying some 'thing' that ought to be accessible to physical or psychological investigation. McFadyen 1990, 313, 318, *et passim*.

Chapter 1

48 See Glover 1988, 23 for the concept of 'doubling', with reference also to multiple personality.

49 Jansz 1991, 262.

50 See Berger 1969, 81.

51 Cf. McFadyen's 'deep "self"' *supra*, n. 46. Cf. Also Cupitt, 'Spirit is only a capacity of persons (a capacity to exceed one's capacities ... a capacity of self transcendence)' 1980, 90. But for Cupitt God is no more than the spirit we become.

52 McFadyen on Barthian lines begins with this assumption: 'since God's communication is the overarching determining and ever-present context within which all personal communication takes place.' (McFadyen 1990, 23). I am closer to Tillich's approach in starting with 'the situation' and the questions it poses.

53 Jansz 1991, 220.

54 See Williams 1985, 281 ff.

2

THE ENRICHMENT OF SACRIFICE

The theme of sacrifice has from the very beginning been at the heart of Christian thinking and talking about Jesus Christ and his saving work, but the question arises over what meaning or meanings sacrifice might have had for Jesus and his followers in the face of his apparent failure and defeat, and what meaning it might have today in a very different world largely unfamiliar with the ritual slaughter of animals. In particular, the question will be raised as to how far the very idea of Jesus' death as a sacrifice carried implications of ultimacy. The account offered here will as far as possible pay regard to the available evidence, but will be somewhat speculative at times in the exploration of possible lines of thought, implicit connections, and the logical outworking of different ideas.

Background

The background to Christian use of the term 'sacrifice' is primarily the Old Testament. What is striking is not only the variety of sacrificial offerings depicted there, but the variety of occasions on which they were to be offered. In early times before the destruction of Jerusalem by the Babylonians in 586 BC and the exile of its leading citizens, various kinds of sacrifice were offered, relating to the Passover, covenant-making, thanksgiving, or communion.[1]

After the exile there was an increasing emphasis on purification rituals, with a climax reached on the Day of Atonement (see Leviticus 16). This preoccupation may be attributed to the prophets' interpretation of defeat and exile as punishment for sin, the breaking of God's covenant, and not due to God's failure.[2] So if the Jews ever returned home again, as they were able to under the Persian King, Cyrus, the Law would have to be kept to maintain the covenant and avoid further disaster.

A problem arises here over the ambiguity of the word 'sin'. It occurs with great frequency in older English translations of Leviticus especially, in relation to rulers, priests or people who contract ritual impurity unawares. This needs to be expiated ('covered', Hebrew *kippur*) by sacrifices usually referred to in the older translations as 'sin offerings'. However, the Revised English Bible (unlike the New English Bible) translates the Hebrew word *chattath* as 'purification offering', accepting that ritual impurity is the issue.

By contrast, E.P. Sanders argues forcefully that the sinners referred to in the Gospels are not the common people or simply those who have infringed the purity code, but are in fact the *resha'im*, the wilfully wicked.[3] A distinction therefore needs to be drawn between two kinds of obstruction preventing access to God, rebellion and impurity. Though the word 'sin' is sometimes used to cover both, to avoid confusion it will be taken here to mean rebellion, the wilful rejection of God's Law.

Impurity resulting from ignorance or accident could be dealt with by the means God had himself provided, namely sacrifice. Most but not all Old Testament sacrifices involved the death of the victim and the shedding of blood in order to expiate sin (impurity). But sacrifice was, it seems, of no avail in expiating deliberate sin (rebellion); the offender must be cut off from the community (Numbers 15:27–36).

However, this extreme conclusion[4] must be qualified. Drawing on rabbinic evidence, Sanders argues that restoration was always possible in Jesus' day if repentance and the desire for forgiveness were present.[5] It is also the case that in the Old Testament there are occasions of sacrifice being offered to atone for deliberate sin, as in the case of Job offering sacrifices for his sons in case they had cursed God (Job 1:5). More significantly, on the Day of Atonement, the climax of sacrificial worship, the High Priest has to offer sacrifices to 'purge the sanctuary of the ritual uncleanness of the Israelites and their acts of rebellion, that is, of all their sins' (Leviticus 16:16 NEB).

Further evidence of the interlocking of rebellion and impurity is seen in pleas for renewal and restoration to fellowship with God couched in the language of ritual purity and so implying a prior state of impurity in relation to wilful sin. This is illustrated in Psalm 51:1, 'Have mercy on me, O God, according to your abundant mercy; blot out my transgressions. Wash me thoroughly from my iniquity, and cleanse me from my sin.' Hence, though impurity is not a sin,[6] it was natural to regard a sinner as impure. Neither sacrificial cleansing nor forgiveness was available for persistent sinners who did *not* repent. It remains the case that both rebellion and impurity barred access to the Temple,[7] and so in a sense to God, though on different grounds.

There is need, then, for a word to cover the two kinds of breach with God. Though somewhat awkward, the word 'unholiness' may serve this purpose and conversely 'holiness' may be taken to embrace both obedience and purity.

Unholiness in the sense of impurity carries connotations of pollution and uncleanness, which is to be avoided if possible. Unholiness in this light is an almost quasi-physical contamination. Thus we read 'Whatever the unclean person touches shall be unclean' (Numbers 19:22). Uncleanness may be unavoidable on occasion, as when a dead body has to be dealt with by next of kin. Even a priest was permitted to defile himself for his closest relatives (cf. Leviticus 21:1–3 and Numbers 19:10b–22). So though impurity or uncleanness was not a sin, nevertheless, it had to be washed away – above all before entering the Temple, to avoid defiling it (cf. Leviticus 15:31).

The other strand of unholiness, rebellion, carries connotations of wilful rejection of God, of disobedience or contempt for the Law. Its converse is not easily captured in a single word, but for simplicity may be called 'moral holiness', signifying a willing obedience to God's Law, or at least the desire to keep it. What must be avoided in this case is not impurity or pollution, but disobedience and wilful rebellion. However, the interchange of imagery leads to rebellious sinners being regarded as unclean. It follows from the logic of ritual holiness that to avoid contamination, the holy people must avoid sinners and not just sin.

Though Sanders argues convincingly that most Jews would not have followed the logic of holiness to an extreme in avoiding the impure, it is significant that some did, such as the Dead Sea community and the *haberim*,[8] while the Pharisees, Sadducees and the common people would all have observed the rules of purity when approaching the Temple.

The convergence of the two strands in the meaning of unholiness is powerfully illustrated in the Day of Atonement ritual described above. Spun together, the two strands of impurity and rebellion give rise to a distinctive concept of unholiness, which to a greater or lesser degree requires the avoidance of the unholy, whether as rebel, or unclean or both, at least for those entering the Temple.

Spiritualization of sacrifice

At the same time as this concentration on sin and impurity occurred, or at least overlapping it, was another significant development, again under

Chapter 2

the impetus of the prophets. This was the so-called 'spiritualization' of sacrifice.[9] The emphasis shifts from the physically pure and spotless victim to the spiritually pure and spotless worshipper, from the objective act of killing an animal with the accompanying blood ritual, towards the subjective inner disposition of the person offering it. A pure life and a faithful death came to be thought of as expiatory. Good deeds, fasting, prayer and the study of the law came to be regarded as the equivalent of sacrifice. Thus to quote Psalm 51 again, 'For you have no delight in sacrifice: if I were to give a burnt offering, you would not be pleased. The sacrifice acceptable to God is a broken spirit; a broken and contrite heart, O God, you will not despise' (Psalm 51:16 f. cf. Psalm 40:6–8).

An interweaving of the spiritual and ritual in sacrifice is found in the Wisdom of Ben Sira (Ecclesiasticus) 35:4–7, 'the one who gives alms sacrifices a thank offering. To keep from wickedness is pleasing to the Lord, and to forsake unrighteousness is an atonement'. But Ben Sira adds 'Do not appear before the Lord empty handed, for all you offer is in fulfilment of the commandment'.

A more radical spiritualization in place of ritual occurs when the traditional rituals were no longer possible, as was the case after the destruction of the Temple by the Romans in AD 70. When Rabbi Joshua lamented the loss of the place of atonement, the Temple, Rabbi Johanan ben Zakkai rebuked him, 'We still have a means of expiation of equal value, the practice of kindness, for it is said, I will have kindness, not offering.'[10]

Similarly, in the Community Rule at Qumran we read, 'For it is through the spirit of true counsel concerning the ways of man that all his sins shall be expiated that he may contemplate the light of life. He shall be cleansed from all his sins by the spirit of holiness uniting him to His truth, and his iniquity shall be expiated by the spirit of uprightness and humility'.[11] We may compare this with Paul in Romans 12:1–2, 'Therefore, my friends, I implore you by God's mercy to offer your very selves to him: a living sacrifice, dedicated and fit for his acceptance, the worship offered by mind and heart' (NEB). However, purification rituals continued at Qumran, especially with water (the Community had withdrawn from the Temple, believing it to have been defiled, and so they could not offer animal sacrifice there).

That the spiritualization of sacrifice was not unique to Judaism is illustrated by an example from the Greek world given by Frances Young,[12] 'The famous philosopher, Socrates, insisted that sacrifice made no difference. Virtue alone was of value in the endeavour to keep the favour of the gods'.

Where such a shift from ritual to righteous living occurs, one might expect the rituals and associated imagery of sacrifice to be abandoned, but that need not happen for reasons to be explored further below, but briefly, it was because scripture would remain authoritative, even if re-interpreted, and rituals could still serve to maintain social solidarity and loyalty to tradition. At issue here are shifts of emphasis, not absolutely exclusive alternatives. Within Judaism obedience to the Law still remained paramount. Thus we find the great platonizing allegorizer, Philo, still insisting on the literal observance of Jewish rites,[13] and although according to Matthew 5:24, 'making peace with your brother' precedes the ritual offering at the altar, the offering was still to be made.

An important factor contributing to the spiritualization of sacrifice, with its emphasis on moral or holy living, would seem to have been an increasing sense of individual responsibility, to which it also contributed.

The emergence of individualism

A tremendous emphasis on moral or spiritual holiness can be seen in the prophets such as Amos 5:21–25 'I hate, I despise your feasts, and I take no delight in your solemn assemblies. Even though you offer me your burnt offerings and your cereal offerings, I will not accept them,... but let justice roll down like waters, and righteousness like an ever-flowing stream'. Amos, like other early prophets, addressed his challenge to the nation (cf. Hosea 6:6, Isaiah 1:10–12). Perhaps this is true also of Jeremiah's furious denunciation of the people's wickedness (Jeremiah 7) but with him and Ezekiel we find a clear assertion of individual responsibility.

'In those days they shall no longer say, "The parents have eaten sour grapes, and the children's teeth are set on edge." But all shall die for their own sins.' (Jeremiah 31:29 f., cf. Ezekiel 18:2).

The Jews, surrounded by the Babylonian army, were blaming their troubles on their fathers' sins. Achan's children in Joshua 7 would have had good reason to do so, and the first commandment would seem to have justified their belief – Exodus 20:5 'I the Lord your God am a jealous God, punishing the children for the iniquity of their parents to the third and fourth generation of those that reject me'. Not so! say Ezekiel and Jeremiah, you are punished for your own sins. Each person is responsible for himself or herself.

This means that within the corporate whole of the Jewish community a distinction is to be drawn between individuals – the righteous and the wicked. Which side to be on depends on individual decision, not on the accident of birth or on what your parents were and did. The more strongly a sense of individuality is felt, the less meaning and importance is likely to be attached to rites and rituals that reflect a sense of corporate identity and help to sustain it.[14] To sum up, the shift towards moral holiness inevitably carries with it an emphasis on individual responsibility, and this inevitably aggravated the problem of suffering.

The problem of suffering
This becomes particularly acute precisely where a sense of individuality is strong, as illustrated by the plaintive protest in Ecclesiastes 2:18 'I hated all my toil in which I had toiled under the sun, seeing that I must leave it to those who will come after me'. The vesting of hope in the nation's future glory is ruled out by such profound detachment from the next generation. Some solution to the problem of suffering must be sought elsewhere.

a. Punishment
One familiar solution (still prevalent) is to see suffering as punishment. It may be unpleasant at the time, but most people would accept that punishment, even if painful, can serve a positive, corrective purpose and so at least be meaningful and even loving, cf. Deut. 8:5. 'Know then in your heart that as a man disciplines his son, the Lord God disciplines you'. (Perhaps Ben Sira went too far in Ecclesiasticus 30:1, 'A man who loves his son will whip him often, so that when he grows up he will be a joy to him').

A very different mood from that of father and child is conjured up by the image of God as a supreme king whose law must be obeyed, else terrible penalties and curses will fall, as in Deuteronomy 28:45 'All these curses shall pursue you and overtake you, because you did not obey the voice of the Lord your God'. Such penalties would seem to be necessary if the credibility of God and his law was not to be undermined, But what sense could it make to punish the innocent and law-abiding? Job agonized about that. His friends argued that suffering is punishment; Job was suffering, therefore he was being punished, therefore he must have sinned (cf. Job 11:4–6). Job insisted he was innocent but found no solution.

For the Jews, the problem of suffering was greatest when the righteous suffered specifically for being righteous, that is, for refusing to break the Law by sacrificing to idols or eating pork. That's what happened in 165 BC under the Greek king, Antiochus Epiphanes, when the wicked who broke God's law and sacrificed to idols, continued to flourish. Well might the Psalmist complain, 'How long, O God, is the foe to scoff? Is the enemy to revile your name for ever?' (Psalm 74:10). What meaning could the suffering of the righteous have? Animal sacrifice would not have shed much light. Suffering as such had no place in it – death and bloodshed, yes, especially bloodshed, but not suffering.

b. Vicarious punishment

There are hints of vicarious intercession in the Old Testament, of pleading on behalf of others, as when Abraham pleads for Sodom (Genesis 18:22–23) and Moses pleads for the people (Numbers 14:11–16). The idea of vicarious death, of dying on behalf of others, scarcely appears except in one striking passage, the Servant Song in Isaiah 53. Here the idea emerges that the innocent might actually be suffering in place of the wicked, to divert the penalties they deserved from them. Who exactly the servant represents remains a mystery, but there are three things to be noticed. First, the servant's death is spoken of as a sacrifice, or more specifically as a guilt offering,[15] *asham*. Is. 53:10 reads 'He made himself an offering for sin'.

But secondly, his death is not literally a sacrifice; the word is clearly metaphorical. Much more is made of an independent theme, that the suffering and ultimate death of a righteous man, God's servant, could be used by God to save others from the penalties of sin. To quote from the NRSV: Isaiah 53:11 'The righteous one, my servant, shall make many righteous, and he shall bear their *iniquities*'(cf. NEB 'himself bearing the *penalty of their guilt*'. The words in italics translate the same Hebrew word, *avon*, as found in Cain's protest in Genesis 4:13 'My punishment is greater than I can bear').

The Isaiah passage goes on to say that the servant will be fully vindicated 'because he exposed himself to face death and was reckoned among the transgressors, because he bore the sin of many and interceded for their transgressions'. There is so much more here than could be attached to or derived from any animal sacrifice, where suffering and punishment played no part. The third point, the ultimate vindication of the servant, could hardly apply to a sacrificed sheep.

The suffering servant featured surprisingly little in later Jewish thought, perhaps because Christians took it over. But the idea of the atoning power of human suffering was developed further, as can be seen in the books of Maccabees.

c. Martyr death as sacrifice

Following the conquests of Alexander the Great, Judea had fallen under

Chapter 2

the control of his successors. Progressive Jews were keen to adopt Greek culture (see 2 Maccabees 4:12) and had the support of the Greek king, Antiochus Epiphanes. However, in what was effectively a civil war,[16] the religious conservatives in the countryside, led by Judas the Hammer (Greek 'Maccabaeus'), fought back fanatically and were unexpectedly victorious.[17]

Before Judas' victory, many Jews preferred to be tortured to death than to betray the Law by eating pork or sacrificing to idols, but their fate posed more acutely than ever the agonising question, Why did God let the wicked apostates flourish and abandon the faithful to cruelty and destruction? That set the scene for profound development in ideas of the atonement and the meaning of sacrifice.

An attempt to make sense of the crisis is found in the books of Maccabees (e.g. 2 Maccabees 7). In the story of the seven brothers and their mother, the old idea that suffering is punishment for sin recurs in verse 32, 'For we are suffering because of our own sins. And if our living Lord is angry for a little while, to rebuke and discipline us, he will again be reconciled with his own servants' (cf. verse 18). We also find hope of resurrection and the vindication of the righteous (verse 14).

The last brother to die returns to the theme of Isaiah 53 with the plea that their extreme suffering and death might suffice for the penalties due for sin so that others may be spared; 'I, like my brothers, give up body and life for the laws of our ancestors, appealing to God to show mercy soon to our nation … and through me and my brothers to bring to an end the wrath of the Almighty that has justly fallen on our whole nation' (2 Maccabees 7:37–38).

In another story in 4 Maccabees 6, the old man Eliazer refuses to eat pork. These words are attributed to him at the point of death, 'Thou O God knowest that though I might save myself I am dying by fiery torments for thy law. Be merciful unto thy people, and let our punishment be a satisfaction in their behalf. Make my blood their purification, and take my soul to ransom their souls'.[18] The implicit interweaving of purity and obedience is striking. The Books of Maccabees can probably be dated between AD 18 and 55.

Such ideas about vicarious atoning sacrifice were not completely unique to Judaism. Martin Hengel[19] alludes to a number of examples. To take one, the Roman author, Lucan, depicts the death of the younger Cato as a sacrifice to atone for the blood guilt of the civil war following Julius Caesar's assassination. Cato addresses Brutus, 'May the barbarians from the

Rhine make me the target of their shots, and exposed to every spear, may I receive all the wounds of the whole war. This my blood will ransom all the people; this my death will achieve atonement for all that the Romans have deserved through their moral decline'. Lucan himself was a contemporary of St Paul. He died probably at the same time on Nero's orders in AD 65 aged 25. As Hengel concludes 'These words help us to understand why the earliest Christian message made sense in Rome'.

But to continue – the problem of suffering is not open to simple explanations, but I would like to suggest a simplified sequence of ideas in six steps (drawing on Peter Berger's concept of 'plausibility crises' which arise when established beliefs or world views are seriously challenged):[20]

- *Set belief*: God is righteous and sovereign
- *Question*: Why then is there suffering? (plausibility crisis)
- *Answer*: Because it is punishment deserved for sin (Job's comforters) or means of discipline (Deuteronomy 8:5) (plausibility restored)
- *Question*: Why do the righteous suffer? (Job asks, plausibility crisis)
- *Answer*: To release others from suffering and punishment due for sin (Isaiah 53; Books of Maccabees) (plausibility restored)
- *Conclusion*: Atonement with a just but ultimately merciful God.

So then, a solution is offered both to the problem of suffering and the problem of sin. Sin is serious, but once the penalty is paid, God's righteousness and holiness is vindicated; the barrier of sin is removed; reconciliation (at-onement) with God is achieved. But there are dangers along this route, if we take it a bit further. Crucial to it is the idea that God accepts the martyr's death as sufficient penalty for sin. It's then only a small step from God accepting to God demanding such penalty, from a merciful God accepting a voluntary offering, to a vengeful God needing to be propitiated, placated, and demanding a horrific penalty to be paid[21] (cf. Daly 1978 p. 35). This is where many people have great difficulty with doctrine of penal substitution; some have questioned whether it has any place in the NT (or at least in Paul) as a way of interpreting Christ's death.[22]

However, it may emerge that though 'penal substitution' may not feature so much in the New Testament as a distinct theme, it is nevertheless drawn into the language of sacrifice through association with martyr death. The convergence of two models of atonement – ritual cleansing by blood and penal death – under the single word, sacrifice, generates a hidden tension within the concept of sacrifice, which is lost if it is interpreted exclusively in terms of one side or the other. The paradoxical two sidedness must, however, be maintained if the fundamental paradox of the Christian faith is to be upheld, namely, that in Christ, God's giving and a human being's responding, together effect reconciliation between God and humanity.

d. Martyr death and the language of sacrifice
The point being argued here is that the idea of martyr death as penalty for sin does not stem from sacrifice, but arises out of the problem posed by the suffering of the righteous. But then the question arises as to why the Hebrew and Greek words for sacrifice are so often used? For three reasons, I suggest:

i. The analogy of outcome
Not the process but the outcome of a martyr's death can be likened to the outcome looked for in animal sacrifice, that is, reconciliation with God. So sacrifice can serve simply as a metaphor or analogy. But there are other stronger reasons for turning to the language of sacrifice.

ii. Martyr death and spiritual sacrifice
Martyr death in obedience to God's law could be seen as the ultimate expression and seal of holy or godly living. We can look at Eliazer again; the author of 4 Maccabees extols him in 7:14–15, 'O blessed age, O reverend grey head, O life faithful to the Law and perfected by the seal of death!' The purity of a holy life, a spiritual sacrifice, is sealed by death; there can now be no apostasy. And the very fact of death would connect again with traditional animal sacrifice as an offering to God, but the word 'sacrifice' would be vastly enriched by the idea of an unblemished human life voluntarily offered up to God, as against a merely physically unblemished sheep being offered by someone else.

To put it the other way round, animal sacrifice falls short of the moral or spiritual, the moral stops short of the limit. In other words, holy living and even holy dying stop short of the voluntary surrender of life in obedience to God, when otherwise it would continue. Martyr death draws the other strands of sacrificial language together and crowns them. It is a profoundly enriched concept of sacrifice that Jesus' disciples (and Jesus himself) could draw on as they tried to interpret his death, but the language they drew on was still that of animal sacrifice and the ritual shedding of blood. We may consider why.

iii. The authority of scripture

I suggest that the *language* of sacrifice came from the Pentateuch, because it had the revelatory authority of sacred scripture, but the clue to its enriched *meaning* is in the Apocrypha and other later writings after the Pentateuch was completed. It is these writings that I believe can shed light on Jesus' and his disciples' way of thinking about atoning sacrifice, but there was also another factor at work. It was still very important for the early Christians to be able to show that Jesus had fulfilled the sacred scriptures.

The need to source everything in the Pentateuch was already a characteristically Jewish concern. The scriptural source for the atoning power of martyr sacrifice was found in the story of the binding of Isaac, the *akedah*, in Genesis 22:29.[23] In later Jewish devotional literature, the *haggadah*, Isaac becomes the ideal martyr and is 'portrayed as a thirty-seven year old man voluntarily acquiescing in the sacrifice', and actually being sacrificed. Hence the *haggadah* speaks of the 'ashes' or 'blood' of Isaac, one version calling him 'the lamb of the burnt-offering'.

Similarly, the early Christians were eager to connect Jesus to the scriptures, but with this difference. His disciples saw him as the fulfilment of the scriptures rather than basing his authority on them. So Jesus is spoken of as the new Adam, the new Moses, the new Joshua (his name), the founder of the new Israel, and in the same vein, the new Temple, new High Priest, new sacrifice (see Hebrews), and, we can add, the new Isaac. These are the types, the shadows; he is the antitype, the reality. But such language does more to *proclaim* that Jesus is the fulfilment of scripture rather than to *explain how* his death makes a difference. Implicit in such a proclamation is the acknowledgement of Jesus' ultimacy.

The question today is whether we are bound to draw on the Old Testament to the same extent. It might in fact be dangerous to do so. We have seen how the ideas of spiritual sacrifice were taken up and sealed in martyr death, while the bare fact of physical death could link martyr death with animal sacrifice. Thus a bridge is created for the interchange of imagery, but the difference between animal sacrifice and the sacrificial significance of martyr death is far greater than the similarities, and this fact can be obscured by the use of the same word 'sacrifice'.

To explain, the interchange of imagery can enlarge and enrich the concept of sacrifice. But there is danger of reverse flow. In other words, instead of the concept of sacrifice being enriched by the death of martyrs, there is a danger of martyr sacrifice being reduced to the level of animal sacrifice, and being interpreted as an external ritual without moral or

Chapter 2

spiritual depth. In other words, the language of animal sacrifice on its own can be dangerously misleading and can literally de-moralize the understanding of Christ and God.

This process can and has lead to quasi-materialistic, sub-personal or magical ideas of how God deals with sin, in complete contrast to the supremely personal understanding of God's relationship to humanity which comes from Jesus himself as portrayed in the New Testament. One reason for this distortion has been the assumption from earliest times that the Old Testament is a direct divine revelation with as much authority as the New Testament.

Later generations have lost sight of the inter-testamental period when the meaning of sacrifice became so enriched. It may be asked now whether the Church has reverted too much, not just to Old Testament language, but to Old Testament ideas of sacrifice (and of priesthood too for that matter, a role that entered scarcely if at all into martyr-death theology).

As an alternative to any quasi-magical view of sacrifice, a more existential approach may offer at least a partial answer to the meaning of sacrifice for today. Faced with a person suffering a cruel death, one can draw one or other of two opposite conclusions. On the one hand, to put it in traditional terms, we can see it as punishment by God. This has a double implication. It distances both God and ourselves from that suffering person – we like to be on God's side.

Conversely, to see a cruel or violent death as a sacrifice is *ipso facto* to see it as acceptable to God. Whatever else sacrifice may mean, it means a death offered to and believed to be acceptable to God. To believe a person's death is acceptable to God is to believe that the person's life, and what he or she died for, is acceptable to God. To see it that way is to see God aligned with that person and that life.

To be on God's side means aligning oneself with that person too, with what he or she lived for and died for, every day and in every place, not just in Temple or Church. Such an existential decision involves a personal re-orientation and ultimate commitment far removed from any crude notions of blood rituals wiping the slate clean in some magical way while one carries on behaving as before.

So to the question, what is the difference between Eliazer's, the suicide bomber's, and Jesus' martyr death? The answer lies in what they died for. Eliazer lived and died for the Law of Moses, the hijackers on September 11th for a perverse distortion of a great tradition. In Tillich's terms, they died for their ultimate concern, proved by their willingness to die for it.

The enrichment of sacrifice

By doing so they reinforced its claims. And Eliazer's fellow Jews certainly saw his death as a sacrifice acceptable to God and an inspiration to those faithful to the Law (cf. 4 Maccabees 6:18–20), and not a punishment he deserved.

Jesus, by contrast, died condemned, it seemed, by the Law of Moses, a man accursed (cf. Galatians 3:13), and thought by some at least to be a blasphemer, or else a threat to the ruling political and religious powers. What did he die for? One can only say, I think, that he died for that vision and experience of God by which and in which he lived, illuminated, certainly, by the Jewish tradition and the Law of Moses, but not completely determined by it.

I suggest that on one crucial point he broke with it. He unravelled the two strands of holiness and abandoned the strand of ritual holiness with its logic of avoidance. Sanders has argued forcibly that observance of the purity code was not a major issue between Jesus and most of his Jewish contemporaries.[24] Impurity was not a sin, as noted above. Even in the case of wilful sinners – the rebellious or wicked – no Jew was likely to have been offended by any action that led to a sinner's repentance and conversion and willingness to keep the Law.[25] However, Sanders identifies a number of reasons why Jesus would have caused deep offence:

> 1. His willingness to befriend sinners who *remained* sinners.[26] His offer of entry to the kingdom of God solely on condition of following him.
> 2. His promise that sinners such as tax gatherers and prostitutes would be given preference in the kingdom of God.
> 3. His implicit and explicit claim to be God's spokesman.[27]
> 4. His challenge to the absolute authority of the Law implied in the above.[28]
> 5. His attack on the Temple.

The last would have offended all Jews, but especially the priestly aristocracy, who alone had the power to secure Jesus' execution and so in Sanders' opinion may be held chiefly responsible for it.[29]

What Sanders does not fully explore are the interconnections of the factors given above.

Re 1: Jesus may well have kept the purity code in everyday matters, but not if it denied him access to the unclean or impure (e.g. lepers) or even to the morally impure wicked. His actions revealed his rejection of the logic of ritual holiness which would have barred such behaviour for fear of contamination.

Re 2, 3 and 4: There was no existing authority to which Jesus could appeal to justify his response to the wicked. So he spoke either for himself, or in the conviction that he spoke for God. Only those willing to follow him and to accept that he spoke and acted for God could grasp what he offered.

Re 5: Apart from the above, an attack on the Temple was a challenge to the Law on which the Temple was based.[30]

Re 6: The Temple was the highly visible, physical and beautiful focus and foundation of a concept of holiness spun out of the two strands of obedience and purity, from which of necessity the wicked and the impure (which included foreigners) were excluded. Whatever the tolerance of impurity elsewhere, ritual purity was essential for entry into the Temple.[31] It stood for a holiness which Jesus in God's name rejected.

By the logic of his own convictions, Jesus was bound to envisage the destruction of the Temple as a condition of the fulfilment of God's ultimate purposes, the inclusion even of the wicked in his kingdom. As Sanders notes, the kingdom Jesus envisaged was *his* kingdom, not God's in the manner of Jewish expectation.[32] Jesus' message was so radical that perhaps we should see his association with the wicked as a powerful prophetic sign in the tradition of the Old Testament prophets. What is clear is that to attack the Temple and to proclaim its destruction would snap the thread of ritual holiness with its logic of exclusion and avoidance of the unholy, whether ritually impure or wilfully rebellious.

Jesus' originality lay in breaking free from the constraint of ritual purity. He would not let anything stand in the way of affirming the disaffirmed. The stories told about him, whether historical or illustrative, reveal the measure of his freedom. He could declare all foods clean and not bother with ritual washing. Much more importantly he was free to touch lepers, to drink from a Samaritan prostitute's cup, and invite himself to eat with a 'polluted' outcast like Zacchaeus, confronting him with a holiness that was not afraid of contamination or pollution. The murmur of disapproval in the crowd in Luke's account of Jesus inviting himself to the house of a notorious sinner, Zacchaeus, may be understood as a sign of the gathering storm (Luke 19:7).

Jesus lived and died for the one he called Father, that was his ultimate concern. He did not die for any book or existing cause. One of his great achievements was never to write a book! By the way he lived and died, Jesus

The enrichment of sacrifice

concretely actualized his ultimate concern. It has been said that we become what we worship. Thus in traditional terms Jesus in his own being revealed God, a God of infinite compassion and unlimited forgiveness. In preferring to be killed than to kill, Jesus revealed a God who would rather surrender his rights for humanity's sake than impose them. One could almost say that God died on the cross and rose again in Jesus. At least, old ideas of God gave way or were transformed in the moment in which Jesus was seen as the revelation of God.

At the same time, in the terms discussed in the last chapter, we can say that Jesus actualized the true potential of human personhood. In that one person the truth of God and of humanity was made visible and real and bodied out in history. Old ideas of God and humanity must take second place where the ultimacy of Jesus is confessed. The sad thing is that Christians have struggled desperately to keep the old ideas despite the difficulty or even the impossibility of fitting them to what must be new. Nowhere has this been more apparent than in debates over how Jesus can be God and man, as though it was a question as to how two incompatible 'things' can be united!

Thus to see Jesus' life and death as a sacrifice acceptable to God is in effect to ascribe an ultimacy to him that takes precedence over any other supposed ultimate or concept of God. The discontinuity with all other claimants is what Marcion[33] and the Gnostics[34] tried to express, but in unsatisfactory ways. But the dangers of overstating the continuity between Jesus and all else are equally real and serious, because there *is* a radical discontinuity. Jesus did pose a challenge to the world of his day and since.

For anyone to make Jesus their own ultimate concern (to see God in him), will not only mean a fresh start like a child, or being born again. It will mean living in the same way as Jesus, and perhaps suffering and even dying for the same reasons. It will also mean a fresh start for God, or at least for God to be seen in a radically new light, a God free to meet and eat with sinners, to embrace the polluted, the unclean, outcasts, gentiles, without fear of pollution or tainted hands, no longer governed by the logic of ritual holiness.

In short, the way is opened up for sinners to be embraced in a relationship with God, a God who proves willing to bear the consequences of sin himself rather than to inflict them on the sinner. In that sense the penalty is indeed paid on our behalf, in our place. Reconciliation is made possible by God, not by human effort. If Jesus, not the Law of Moses, is ultimate, then the Law's condemnation is no longer absolute; instead Jesus'

Chapter 2

acceptance of all is absolute. Faith in his ultimacy is not only a matter of commitment, but a matter of trusting him, and the God seen in him, to be on our side.[35]

To work out the implications of Jesus' ultimacy for human understanding is the task of theology. To work out the implications for living is the task of Christian ethics. The tasks are distinct but belong together. Both must rest on the conviction that Jesus' life and death was truly sacrificial, acceptable to God. Such a conviction embraces the paradox at the heart of all Christology, namely, that Jesus was at once God and human, the true revelation of God in his true humanity (not at the expense of it). As such he could be seen as the God-given means to wipe out sin through the free offering up of himself in his humanity to the source of love and life whom he called 'Father'.

The next question to be explored is what sense can we make today of the idea of Jesus as saviour and how might the traditional doctrines of atonement and redemption be interpreted today in the light of the approach I have adopted.

Notes

  1 Young 1975. Cf. Daly 1978.
  2 Ibid., 27.
  3 Sanders 1985, ch. 6.
  4 Young 1975, 27.
  5 Sanders 1985, 202.
  6 Ibid., 183.
  7 See Sanders 1985, 182.
  8 Cf. Sanders 1985, 181, 'The *Haberim* were lay people who maintained themselves in a relatively high state of ritual purity.'
  9 Young 1975, 35.
  10 Ibid., 34.
  11 Vermes 1975, 75.
  12 Young 1975, 38.
  13 See Young 1975, 45.
  14 Douglas 1970, 14, 'The better defined and the more significant the social boundaries, the more bias I would expect in favour of ritual' and so vice versa.
  15 The distinction between sin and guilt offerings is much debated. Perhaps Leviticus 7:7 offers the best solution, 'The guilt offering is like the sin offering, there is one law for them.'
  16 Cf. Hengel 1974, 277 ff.
  17 Comparison might be made with Ayotolla Khomeini's victory over the

American backed Shah of Iran.
  18 Charles (ed.) 1913, vol. ii, 674.
  19 Hengel 1981, 24.
  20 Berger 1969, 45.
  21 The Septuagint translation of Leviticus 17:11 suggests a wrathful punishing God not found in the Hebrew. Cf. Daly, 34 f.
  22 Cf. Whiteley 1964, 147 (at least in respect of Paul).
  23 See Daly, 48.
  24 Sanders 1985, 199.
  25 Ibid., 272.
  26 Ibid., 206, 267, 269.
  27 Ibid., 280, 293.
  28 Ibid., 280, 301.
  29 Ibid., 293.
  30 Ibid., 267.
  31 Ibid., 182, 'Most purity laws, however, are not prohibitions; they do not require people to avoid impurity. They regulate, rather, what must be done after contracting impurity *in order to enter the* temple (emphasis original). Cf. 186.
  32 Ibid., 206 ff.
  33 Marcion was condemned as a heretic for radically divorcing the just, creator God of this world, giver of the Law to Moses, from the good God revealed for the first time in Jesus Christ. See Kelly 1977, 57.
  34 For Gnostics, cf. ch. 5, n. 24.
  35 Cf. Tillich 1978, ii, 179, 'Man must accept that he is accepted. He must accept acceptance.'

3

REDEMPTION AND RECONCILIATION IN CHRIST[1]

The setting of the question of the atonement
Why should the life and the cruel death of a Galilean holy man two thousand years ago have any significance today in our vastly different world? How can it do any good to me, let alone to humanity in general, in the face of all the disruptive and destructive forces let loose in the world? Paul spoke of it at the time as a scandal to Jews and foolishness to Greeks (1 Cor. 1:23). It has now become highly problematic for historians, a source of indignation to cultural pluralists, and to many others a matter of supreme indifference. In the last case, it is not because our world is any less threatened or disordered than it was in Jesus' day. It must rather be because the connections between his life and ours have somehow been lost. It is left to a few who are seemingly out of touch with the world as it 'really' is to harp on about Jesus, while those who are in touch feel, with more or less regret, that questions about Jesus are not now worth pursuing seriously.

Arthur Lyttleton argued in *Lux Mundi* for the inter-connection of doctrine:

> Theological doctrine, describing as it professes to do, the dealings of an all-wise Person with the human race, must be a consistent whole, each part of which reflects the oneness of the will on which it is based. What we call particular doctrines are in reality only various applications to various human conditions of one great uniform method of divine government which is the expression in human affairs of one Divine will.[2]

Such confidence in divine government might have carried more conviction in the nineteenth century than it would for many now, but on one point at least Lyttleton is correct. No doctrine can be properly understood in isolation, least of all the doctrine of the atonement, precisely because the word means 'reconciliation'. It has to with interaction, the drawing

Chapter 3

together of what has fallen apart. That used to mean primarily, humanity and God. But few are bothered now about Adam and Eve's disobedience or the God that they offended. Far more real is the anguished experience of one's own life, of relationships falling apart, of society divided and nations in conflict. Humanity itself seems to be at war with the natural order. The values and beliefs that once guided us and gave meaning to life are, it seems, broken beyond repair. The stories that used to enchant us are now so much bric-a-brac around our feet like the children's toys; we cannot bring ourselves to throw them out and yet do not know what to do with them. The question of atonement is whether these and the many other scattered fragments of existence can be drawn together into wholeness – a wholeness that is not a plaything but life-enhancing power.

Lyttleton notes that 'In the course of religious controversy this doctrine [of atonement] has become separated from the rest, at one time neglected, at another over emphasized, till in its isolation it has been so stated as to be almost incredible' . His worthy aim was to restate it in a manner consistent with its wider doctrinal setting and in terms that could make sense to the beliefs and experiences of his day. Precisely because the question of atonement is so remote from the beliefs and experiences of so many in our day, it is tempting to settle for the narrower task of relating it simply to its wider doctrinal setting. For people who are still at home in its traditional setting, this remains a useful and necessary undertaking. Those who have no difficulty with the idea of God as an 'all-wise Person' are rightly still concerned to exclude what is incredible and unworthy of God in Christian doctrine. A firm basis for this undertaking is provided by the beliefs that Jesus Christ is the incarnate Son of God and that the sacred scriptures are the inspired witnesses to God's revelation in him. Yet it is beliefs such as these in their traditional formulations that for many raise an impenetrable barrier between Jesus and themselves, between Jesus as he is portrayed and talked about and the world as we experience it and perceive it in a scientific age. The tension between the two has contributed to the collapse of doctrinal confidence which renders the wider doctrinal setting itself as shaky as a partly dismantled scaffolding – no longer the secure framework in which to reconstruct the doctrine of atonement or any other doctrine.

Ways of proceeding
In these circumstances, two basic options are open: one is to fend off the modern world and modern thought at every point and to declare in God's

name that nothing ever can or ever will disturb the frame of traditional doctrine. Only time will tell if this is so; discussion is fruitless. The second option is to embark on the difficult task of doctrinal reconstruction, in which each attempt to reformulate one doctrine may, indeed must, involve reformulations of all the others, if they are to fit together coherently. This means that the second option is not a single option at all, because every attempt to reconstruct will give rise to a different framework. Since the value of each cannot be settled until the different possibilities have been tried and tested, it follows that a time of doctrinal reconstruction must be a time of doctrinal pluralism.

Pluralism as such is not new in the case of the atonement, since the Church never ascribed dogmatic authority to its teaching on this subject. What is new is not only the need to reformulate it within the wider setting of doctrinal reconstruction, but to do so in the context of very different understandings of the function of language that have emerged over time. Recognition of the pictorial and symbolic function of language (not only in theology) loosens the hold of rigidly defined propositions. This opens up possibilities of repicturing and resymbolizing the realities with which theology is concerned in a way that is at once more tentative and less exclusive than were the formulations of the past. Those who yearn for unshakeable security may see the loosening of language and the diversification of frameworks as a sign of weakness. For others it is a sign of strength and courage. Whatever their value, it is not structures or terminology that matter, whether doctrinal or otherwise, but human beings. A framework of belief and understanding within which a person can grow becomes a prison or a cage when it cannot be changed or enlarged. In the process of change mistakes may be made, but human beings open to each other and to the quest of truth can help each other to keep such mistakes to a minimum. In other words, within the option of doctrinal pluralism, argument, misunderstanding, and indeed passionate disagreement may arise, but from it truth may be hammered out, not as a finished product but as a way of life. For all the variety, the connecting thread will be the conviction that this way of life is not a merely speculative possibility or purely human achievement, but something made real for, and available to, all human beings through the life and death of Jesus.

Given that the task of formulating a single fully adequate doctrine of atonement is ruled out for the reasons offered above, we can with some relief settle for the lesser task of trying to show how the story of Jesus and the events surrounding him may still speak with transforming and integrating power to ourselves and our world. This needs to be done in terms that are compatible with, though not necessarily determined by, modern perceptions of the world. It may also emerge that ways of understanding and responding to that story today do in fact express the underlying intentions of earlier interpretations. Though the temptation to find present day thinking in the past for the sake of doctrinal respectability must be resisted, this does not mean that a continuity of experience and understanding has to be ruled out. After all, it would be surprising if this continuity were totally lacking in human beings in any age whose lives are orientated on Jesus, even if deep gulfs of time and thought separate them.

Facing up to the difficulties
The problem for many today in relation to the doctrine of the atonement is that key words have lost their power. Sin is out of fashion, the Devil a joke, and God irrelevant. Of course that is not universally the case, but even where such terms have not lost all seriousness, they are often used ambivalently or superstitiously. Problems have long been recognized within traditional theological discourse. How is it that a loving omnipotent God could have allowed the Devil such scope for destruction for so long? How can victory be claimed when evil is still so rampant in the world? Again, if God is loving, why could he not have offered us free forgiveness without demanding satisfaction on our behalf, or the punishment of his innocent Son in our place, or a sacrifice for sin whatever that may mean; and why is there so much suffering?

Apart from attempting to reinstate such language and imagery with all its problems, we may try to meet the difficulties in two ways. One is to accept this traditional terminology but to reconsider its function. The other would be to abandon it in favour of other terms that may better express for us what is at stake.

Taking myth seriously[3]
The first solution to the embarrassment caused by the bizarre imagery of the atonement is to stop being embarrassed and to acknowledge unashamedly its mythological character. 'Myth' must be understood here not as a fairy tale or outdated pre-scientific *explanation* of how things are, but in the very positive sense of a story that *declares* how things are and by so doing makes them what they are for the hearer who receives it. Thus myths function positively as reality-constituting stories.

Redemption and reconciliation in Christ

A myth can be false if it portrays things wrongly and so misleads. A myth is true if it discloses and communicates to the hearer what is real. In so doing it illuminates even if it does not explain. The point can be illustrated from Kipling's *Just So* story about the Elephant Child and the crocodile, even if this is only a pseudo-myth. The fact is that elephants do have long trunks and crocodiles long jaws, even if there was no tug-of-war on the banks of the Limpopo river at the dawn of history. The story is simply untrue if regarded as history, or as literal description of events, or as scientific explanation. But it communicates truths in its conclusion which might be of more value to a child living by the Limpopo than any amount of theoretical knowledge about Darwin and evolution.

A story, whether told out of imagination or derived from historical events, acquires mythological power when it serves to impart and so create an understanding of reality in the mind of the hearer. Fundamental myths not only declare what the world is like, but where human beings belong within the totality of things. The myth that matters to me is the story that tells me where I am in the vastness of reality – where I come from and where I am going, who I am and what I might be. Seen from outside, it is just one of many stories that jostle for attention in the crowded bazaar of reality seekers. Whether these stories are labelled political, ideological or religious, they are all addressed to similar needs. Seen from inside, the story I grasp, or rather that grasps me, is the one that makes me and my world, my visions and my hopes, what they are. Though vital to me it cannot be my private property; rather it is shared by and communicated to me by the community I belong to, whether I was born into it or drawn or driven into it in later life.

The stories Christians told of old and still sing about declare that we as human beings have grounds for hope and joy because there is something or rather someone ultimately real and powerful who is on our side. It is indeed no accident that these stories are most powerfully evocative in the setting of the cult, rather than in the lecture hall. They celebrate the 'truth' that is believed and lived within, against the backdrop of what might have been otherwise. God might have been helpless against the power of evil, the Devil; or he might not have been on our side, but a demon or cosmic joker playing cat and mouse with human beings before destroying them; or he might ultimately have been a God of Law who could not or would not revoke the penalties due to law breakers – eternal damnation. Indeed, there might be no ultimate God, only an empty void in which the cry of humanity is no more than momentary disturbance of infinite silence.

Chapter 3

Stories that end with the declaration that there is God and that he is as he is seen to be in Jesus, and that what is ultimately real is the relationship we have with God through Jesus, are Christian myths, in the most positive sense of myth as the story that declares who we are and where we stand. To accept it as true is to believe that the story does not simply make things what they are by merely saying it, but that by saying it, it imparts and makes true and real for the hearer what is real and true in itself. Grasping and being grasped by the story is faith in its twofold character as gift (grace) and decision. However bizarre the imagery sometimes used in the story, the crucial point is that things are as the final conclusion declares them to be. Whether there is a Devil or not, whatever the forces of evil may be, God is not powerless against them, nor is he against us.

Moving from what seems more obviously mythological, such as conflicts with the Devil, one might also say that many ostensibly rational theories of atonement – of satisfaction or penal substitution – are mythologically valid, that is, truth-imparting, if in their conclusion they impart a message of hope through Christ, however logically inadequate or morally repugnant they may appear in the telling. The worst mistakes follow from treating them as proofs or explanations throughout, rather than as declarations in their conclusions.

Demythologising – the existential way
However, it will not do just to take myth seriously and leave it at that, for two reasons. First, the Christian story is not simply an imaginative account of what might have been, but is about things that really happened to real people – a story grounded in history, in a personal life, and in the impact of that life on other human lives. The fact that this story acquired mythological – reality-constituting – power can be fully acknowledged, but unless the manner in which mythological significance was woven into the account of historical events is clearly perceived, serious and dangerous distortion can result, as when historical elements are mistaken for mythological, and vice versa.

The danger of transposing historical actors on to the stage of mythological drama can be illustrated by the traditional portrayal of Cowboys and Indians. Historically, there was conflict between European immigrants and indigenous peoples in North America. The story of their encounter and conflict served mythologically to help forge the identity of white Americans, as brave heroes conquering a hostile environment. But casting the indigenous peoples of America in the mythological role of demonic forces opposed to the triumph of virtue grotesquely misrepresented their humanity and served to distort history.

We may now see that a similar fate befell the Jews when the story of Jesus acquired mythological significance. Their role in history was to be members of a society that reacted variously and ambiguously to the challenge presented by the appearance of a fellow Jew called Jesus. If they have any role in the mythological presentation of the ensuing drama, it is as representatives of humanity, not excluding Christians, when confronted by the truth of God. When the mythological and historical role of the Jews is confused, the consequences have been and still are appalling. (It is no accident that the danger manifested itself in the earliest writings to dwell on the historical events of Jesus' life, i.e. in the Gospels, and is less evident in Paul, a writer who dwelt more on its aftermath.)

Secondly, to treat doctrines as myth and no more is in any case to do them less than justice. It may safeguard them as declarations of faith, and yet simply of blind faith, without any explanatory value or rational appeal. To leave faith unsupported by any rational or intellectual framework is to leave it liable to collapse or open to unwitting absorption into portrayals of reality fundamentally at odds with the origins and intentions of Christian faith.

To recognize the unsupported character of faith and to do nothing about it may initially be mistaken for heroic reliance on faith alone; in fact it is evidence of irresponsible laziness and of a refusal to face up to the struggle of seeing how faith must relate to our understanding and experience, if it is to enhance and not exclude human reason. To exclude human reason would not only result in split consciousness, but would be an insult to God's creation.

In any case, the fact that the story of Jesus had a before and after in the flow of history means that the conclusion of his story cannot be totally divorced from the structure and setting of the whole. The problem for us, as we have seen, is that the original conceptual framework of that whole was a pre-scientific picture of reality which inevitably clashed and still clashes with modern scientific perceptions of the world. It is these considerations that drive us towards the alternative route proposed above.

The route we have explored was that of accepting traditional language and imagery but of re-evaluating and restricting it to a mythological function. The alternative to be pursued now is that of finding different terms and imagery that point to the disruption and disorder in the experience of individuals and society, but which have emerged within and so are compatible with scientific perceptions of human life and the world in a way in which many of the old images are not. Such terms are 'alienation', 'estrangement' and 'inauthentic existence'. The task then for the doctrine of atonement will be to try to show how Jesus' life and death has or somehow can overcome these things and put humanity right, drawing together the scattered aspects of life.

Those who pursue this line will face two questions. First, how truly is 'God' in word and reality involved in the situation that is analysed in 'ungodly' language? Is God being adapted to fit into the human reconstruction, or does the human reconstruction and the analysis of human experience in fact help to disclose where and how God is actually at work?

Secondly, is 'sin', too, being adapted to fit into the human reconstruction? or does the reconstruction based on the analysis of human experience in fact help to disclose something of the true quality and character of sin? We have already noted in the last chapter how different understandings of sin are to be found. The question now arises as to how far different terms can function adequately as synonyms for 'sin', or whether that word signifies something distinct which cannot be set aside in theology.

A familiar word for this transposition of imagery, though one that has often proved misleading, is 'demythologization'; It is misleading here because it employs 'myth' in a sense contrary to that which was offered in the previous section. Rudolf Bultmann commonly used the word 'myth' in a derogatory sense (similar to 'discourse' in Martin Heidegger's philosophy) for a way of speaking which objectified dimensions of reality which were not objects, such as human existence, God, life as a continuing open process, love itself. His programme of demythologization was therefore an attack[4] on false objectifications which barred the way to the real encounter between human beings and the will of God disclosed in Jesus. This has nothing to do with the idea of myth explored above as a reality-constituting story. To avoid the risk of confusion arising from different meanings of 'myth', Paul Tillich preferred to speak of 'deliteralization' rather than 'demythologization', and so to preserve 'myth' as a possible vehicle of truth rather than inevitably of untruth, as usually in Bultmann's usage. Whether the word 'myth' is abandoned or reinterpreted, the intention here is the same, to escape from the literalistic, quasi-scientific objectivist understanding of traditional imagery, and in the case of atonement language, to recover its value as the symbolic declaration of renewed relationship with God and the recovery of human wholeness.

However, Bultmann's aim was to go further than this and to engage in the task of transposing traditional Christian doctrine into contemporary language, in particular into the terminology and to some extent the conceptuality developed by Heidegger. For this reason, his project has sometimes been described as an exercise in remythologization or doctrinal reconstruction, using the tools of existentialist philosophy developed by Heidegger to recover the truth-imparting quality of the story of Jesus, where truth has to do with life and meaning, rather than with objective facts.

This is not the place to give an elaborate account of Bultmann's reconstruction, but some key elements of it should be mentioned. For a start, though he is commonly spoken of as an 'existentialist', both he and Heidegger may be better described as phenomenologists in so far as they analyse the concrete experience of human existence and reflect upon the conditions that make it possible. Such reflection discloses human beings as existing uniquely between the sheer givenness of things and the freedom of decision, that is, between or within the polarities of facticity and possibility. Thus reflection discloses human finitude and confronts the human being with the challenge to accept his or her freedom in the face of death, to accept finitude. In Heidegger's words, human existence is being-towards-death.[5]

To recognize this fact is to live authentically. But human beings are tempted to run away from the fact of death – the limitation on their freedom – and to hide from the responsibility and guilt which their freedom confers. In short, they fall into inauthentic existence. The question of salvation, then, is the question of the power to live authentically, of how to escape from the loss of self in the irresponsibility of the collective, from the loss of subjectivity in the world of objects. For Bultmann, in opposition to Heidegger, this power is not innate in the call of conscience, but is given, a gift of grace through the preaching of the Word of God. In that preaching two possibilities of human existence are disclosed, of turning away from or of turning towards Jesus as the revealer of the will of God. In making the cross of Christ their own, believers discover liberation from the powers of this world, the law, sin and death.

The experience of the gift is in effect a pre-emptive victory over death, and entry into true authentic life. Traditional Christian imagery of fall, sin, damnation, of the Devil, and of Christ's atoning work and resurrection can all then be reinterpreted along these lines, no longer as descriptions of objectified beings or external events, but as the symbolic representation of existential experience, the transposition from inauthentic to authentic existence through encounter with the Word of God. For many this approach has breathed new life into outworn symbols and made sense of the (at face value) unbelievable accounts of God's dealings with forces of sin and disorder in human experience.

Two things stand out of this brief summary: first, the intervention of God in the world is narrowed down to the impact of the Word on the depths of the individual. This may appear to have advantages and disadvantages. On the one hand, no embarrassing competition arises between God and the structures of causality open to empirical scientific observation. On the other hand, it may seem that too much has been sacrificed for such a gain – the sense of God's providential guidance and of his being the one who answers prayer and is present in a loving relationship. Secondly, in the nature of the existentialist approach, the emphasis is on the individual. It is this that offends the proponents of the view that human life is best approached and understood in terms of the solidarities and structures of corporate existence, not in its isolated particulars. It is to reconstructions from this perspective that we now turn.

The social way
The Bible witnesses to the continuous warfare of the prophets against idols and false gods from the time of the golden calf (Exodus 32). It has often been remarked that Karl Marx stands in this tradition, extending the campaign against idolatry from constructs of wood and stone to the constructs of society, both its political and economic structures and its conceptual systems. His analysis was subsequently developed in two related but distinct directions; put simply, the political and the sociological – in particular, in the sociology of knowledge.

It can be argued that in the task of doctrinal reconstruction theologians today have as much right to draw on Marxist analysis as Paul had to draw on Judaism, the early Christians on Plato, Aquinas on Aristotle, or Bultmann on Heidegger. The biggest difference perhaps is that, in the nature of the case, an analysis utilizing Marxist tools is likely to hit traditional views where it hurts most, by targeting not merely theoretical constructions, but the power base and material interests of the constructors or defenders of those constructions. The threat posed is especially acute since analysis alone is deemed invalid unless it is the fruit of action, or praxis, of a kind likely to impinge directly on vested interests. A further threat to theoretical constructions is posed when critical analysis radically challenges their claim to absolute or revelatory status, and in consequence the threat extends to the authority of whatever systems they have hitherto served to legitimate.

Thus doctrinal reconstruction in the light of Marxist analysis, not least the reconstruction of the doctrine of the atonement, has had an unavoidable practical and political impact, as seen in South America, where it has emerged most strongly in liberation theologies. These threaten traditional ecclesiastical authorities, not only because of their political character, but because they stem from the rejection in principle of the traditional doctrinal structure of those authorities.

Again, this is not the place to go into the details of Marxist analysis, or Liberation Theology, but in brief, a central feature is the belief that socio-economic and political systems are not natural, neutral or God-given phenomena, but the result of the modes and relations of production which in turn give rise to the class structure and the conflict of class interest. In the struggle for advantage between the classes, ideas and belief systems, not excluding religious belief systems, become the ideological tools of those in power; in other words, they serve to protect and legitimate their particular interests. Whether one thinks of the proletariat or the powerless in a broader sense, the underdogs in the class struggle are denied the achievement of truly human existence and thus experience alienation in its harshest form.

The victims of alienation are enslaved in this situation as long as they suppose their condition to be natural or God-given, in other words, unchangeable and not the result of human activity. The first step to liberation, wholeness, and salvation is to know that the alienating and enslaving system is not absolute. What humans have made they can unmake. The god revealed as an idol can be overthrown, its demonic power broken. But this discovery comes about through challenging action and not merely by theorizing.

What 'liberation' or 'salvation' means in this context is a crucial question for the Christian theologian. Are such concepts being transposed into socio-political terms without remainder in such a way as to part company with the Christian tradition? This is the fear of many (not least in the Vatican), and is one reason for opposition to Latin American theology. On the other hand, it can be argued that any insight into the causes of dehumanization and into ways of overcoming it belongs by right to the religion of incarnation and redemption and can even recall it to its proper task when it has failed.

Chapter 3

Before exploring how these ideas might contribute to a Christian doctrinal reconstruction, we should consider the other stream of thought flowing from the same original source, the sociological. The crucial insight of the sociology of knowledge is the recognition that not only socio-political systems but conceptual systems, world views or cognitive structures, are human social products and not autonomous or God-given.[6] In fact, the belief that any world view is absolute or God-given is taken to be a symptom of alienation, which is precisely the result of human beings forgetting that their world view is the product of society, that is, of many generations interacting with their environment and each other in the search for order and meaning and indeed survival The resultant world view or cognitive structure confronts the community in the present as something given to it from outside, hence 'alien' and not the fruit of its own labour.

However, the function of a world view in establishing order and meaning is so vital that any challenge to it will create a plausibility crisis (to use Berger's expression); the price of changing it, let alone abandoning or overthrowing it, can seem too great to contemplate. It becomes the task of the authorities, supported by the guardians of sacred tradition – the priesthood – to defend the prevailing world view against any challenge. Yet in so far as any given world view is not absolute or perfect, its relation to the realities of existence will be increasingly strained as time passes in a changing world (even the most accurate map becomes unreliable in time). The attempt to maintain its authority will prove increasingly destructive for human society, however sincere the motives of its defenders. But, as noted above, sincerity is no substitute for truth, and even that sincerity may well be doubted if on closer examination it turns out that it is the defenders' interests and power that is legitimated by such a system and threatened by the loss of its divine or quasi-divine authority.

In so far as inauthentic existence or alienation in a political or conceptual sense is dehumanizing, the overcoming of these conditions must clearly be a first step on the path to humanization (the achievement of personhood). What follows will then depend on what is meant by truly human, or what sort of quality, value or goal is presupposed in the project of becoming human. It is here that Christianity may prove to be distinctive, even if it employs the analysis of non-Christians in arriving at an understanding of what it is to be somehow less than truly human and why that state has come about. If the story of the fall of Adam and Eve is not taken literally, an answer to the latter question – why we are less than fully human – must at least be attempted. In so far as the questions concern the actual condition of all human beings, we may reasonably look to our fellow human beings for a contribution to the answer, even if more adequate understanding awaits the discovery of the true solution to the problem. It is here that the paths may and do divide over the question whether human beings individually or corporately have it within themselves to put themselves right, or whether they in fact depend on some source beyond themselves for the possibility of being righted. These questions are too big to be settled here, but our next step will be to examine how Jesus' life and death may be understood against the framework of thought briefly summarized in this section, and how the traditional imagery of atonement might be understood in a reconstructed framework.

Jesus – the odd one out
In terms of the account of alienation given above, Jesus stands out strikingly as a man without a power base, not representing or defending group interests, unless one can say he defended the 'group interest' of the poor, social outcasts, and the weak, but their plight was in large part not to be a group. In what sense would a rich quisling tax official count himself in the same group as a leper? or a successful insider dealer with an AIDS victim or starving refugee? (Some recent theology has perhaps been too ready to align Jesus with the poor as a group.) Further, he lacked recognized authority (see Matthew 21:23–27). Yet he spoke with authority and by so doing presented an inescapable challenge to the existing range of recognized authorities, whether religious or political or both.

Jesus posed a threat to the imperial Roman procurator who had reason to fear the appearance of a Messiah, i.e. any nationalist leader who appeared challenge the power of Rome. A man who denied the absolute authority of any worldly power could easily and however misleadingly be lumped in with the Jewish nationalists and enemies of Rome whose policies of violence posed a serious threat to Roman interests. At the same time, a Jesus who challenged the authority and status of the Pharisees and Sadducees could easily be cast in the role of enemy of God, the Temple, and the Torah (or 'Law of Moses'), which they claimed to defend and on which their authority was based. If Jesus truly spoke for God, his authority would have to be acknowledged. It is not surprising that many considered this unthinkable; it was much easier to suppose he was a rebel or a blasphemer, who should be treated accordingly.

Chapter 3

These were not the only group interests that failed to control Jesus or hitch him to their cause. According to the New Testament, he slipped out of the clutches of public opinion when the crowd tried to make him king (John 6:15). He declared himself free from family ties in a way that was remarkable for a Jew (Mark 3:31–35). He pursued what he saw to be his own vocation even when pressed to do otherwise by his closest friends and advisors (Mark 1:36–38; Luke 1:51–56). He accepted what in historical terms one could see as the inevitable outcome, his rejection by all vested and group interests, and finally a cruel death.

It is a profound paradox that what in worldly terms is the final denial of freedom was in the case of Jesus the final manifestation of freedom. Death came to him because he refused to become anyone else's property or tool; he was his own man, or should we say God's man? It might be objected that to mention God here is to reintroduce the old doctrinal structure from which we are trying to escape, but that is to go too far. The task of doctrinal reconstruction is not to deny God but to ask how we may conceive of the relation of God, as the ultimate ground of life and reality, to our own world and existence as we now perceive and experience it.

To be confronted by one who is free, who is true to himself in the face of the forces of alienation and inauthentic existence, is to be challenged by the question, How could he be like that? Was his freedom and humanity the fruit of the heroic exercise of his own innate resources, in short, his own achievement? Or was it because his refusal to put his trust in unreliable worldly powers (to worship idols) left him open to the gift of life-giving power from which all existence ultimately derives and by which it is sustained? In other words, we might be able to say that by not aligning himself with anything or anyone else, he was able to be and to remain perfectly aligned with God, and in doing so to be free, authentic, unalienated, able to demonstrate how death and all that corrupts and dehumanizes can be defeated by the power of life, which even the fact of physical death could not overcome.

The sheer phenomenon of Jesus challenges us with these questions, however sure or unsure we may be of the answers. Luckily, we do not need to have all the answers in order to make a choice. The choice indeed is unavoidable. Confronted by Jesus' way of being in the world, as conveyed to us by the Gospel stories and the lives of his followers, Do we align ourselves with him or not? No one can dictate the choice to anyone else, but one can spell out the implications.

Defeat of the devil and accomplices

To align oneself with Jesus, to respond to his way of being human in the world, is *ipso facto* to withdraw recognition from the claim of anyone or anything else to be ultimate or determinative. In so far as we ever regarded anyone or anything else explicitly or implicitly to be ultimate, we recognize now that we were worshipping an idol,[7] a false god, and so were guilty of sin against God. In contemporary terms, in so far as anything we once regarded as ultimate or absolute is now seen to be a worldly phenomenon or a human creation, whether a political, cultural, religious or conceptual construct, then in principle the state of alienation is overcome and its destructive consequences are held in check. In practice, the followers of Jesus are unlikely to achieve or experience immediate and complete release from alienation and its subtle hold upon their lives (as Paul knew well). They were and still are no more exempt than Jesus was himself from the externally destructive power of individuals and societies still in the grip of alienation in the world. It means rather that the power of alienation to take hold of and corrupt our innermost being and to drive us towards the corruption and destruction of others, is ultimately broken.

It is in these terms that the traditional imagery of victory over the Devil can be understood. The Devil here is not an autonomous agent of evil whose interference in the world is problematic on every count, but the symbol and symptom of human godlessness, the destructive power unleashed when human beings make what is less than God their God. God's apparent failure to destroy the Devil proves to be an act of grace, given that the destruction of the Devil could only mean the destruction of human freedom to turn from God, and hence equally, the loss of human freedom to turn to God in love. We may hold that the freedom of human beings to turn to God in love is co-extensive with their freedom to turn to each other in love and thus the precondition of becoming human in community.

The question for Christian faith

The greatest challenge of all faces religious people; they are familiar with God-talk and recognize the unqualified seriousness of claims made for God and of claims believed to be made by God on human beings. The hardest false God of all to overthrow is the one we have always believed to be the true God. Easygoing agnostics are not bothered, but the price to be paid for principled not bothering is to deny seriousness to existence. The price to be paid by those who do bother is to face the risk of taking the wrong thing too seriously. It is no accident that in his day those who bothered most about God were most bothered about Jesus. Yet we need to remind ourselves that bothering too much about God can all too easily become a cloak for bothering too much about ourselves.

To take Jesus' side is to deny the claim to absolute seriousness (that is, the name of God) to anything else but Jesus. Yet Jesus addressed another as God. Here lie the roots of Christian reflection about God that leads ultimately to the doctrine of the Trinity. That is not an issue to be pursued just yet. We ask rather, if God is truly seen in Jesus, what follows?

The negative side, as we have seen, though it is hardly negative, is release from false absolutes of our own or society's making. Both are important. The desire in all of us to give content and shape to the ultimate mystery of being results in a cottage industry of God production, of little dolls grandly dressed and cherished too long after we should have grown up and come to grips with reality. Whatever an individual thinks or believes about God needs to be constantly challenged and tested against the words of scripture, the formative insights of tradition, the experience and perception of fellow Christians and indeed of all our fellow human beings in their search for truth in every area of life. Even if it stands the test for a time, no single product or expression of human thought about God can claim to be absolute and eternally binding without becoming an idol, and imposing the shackles of alienation upon us. For creating our own idols we are responsible. God is always more than we can say.

But we are part of a society or societies that are engaged in the same enterprise. And here often more is at stake; the gods of society offer security and power to their worshippers and defend their interests. To challenge these, as Jesus knew well, is a dangerous exercise. Those who are aligned with him are committed to deny all other claims to ultimacy. It falls to them to challenge the powerful, whose aim is to enforce those claims, wherever they conflict with the vision that stems from Jesus of what it means to be human in the world. To spell out that vision adequately here or anywhere is impossible, it is still in the process of being worked out in history, but it has everything to do with life and freedom, with drawing human beings out of the narrow confines of subhuman, degrading, fettered conditions (whether of body or spirit) into the maturity of personhood bonded by love and enhanced by self sacrifice. This can never be a perfect state on earth, but confronts humanity as a project always to be pursued, whatever the cost, because it conforms with the purpose of creation.

Redemption and reconciliation in Christ

The vindication of such sweeping statements does not lie in the quality or otherwise of the language in which they are expressed but in the actualization, even if imperfect, in living experience of what is so described. It is to the extent that such a vision becomes a reality in the lives of those who respond to Jesus, and can be seen to be real by others, that the claim to truth may be vindicated – by their fruit you shall know them (cf. Matthew 7:20).

The question of other faiths
The claim to possession of a truth that is valid and significant for all human beings raises one of the most challenging questions facing Christianity today; How does it stand in relation to the great religions of the world and their claims to truth? This will be pursued further in chapter 6. In the confines of this chapter only two brief points may be made.

First, nothing said thus far would preclude acknowledgement of truth and value in other faiths. It cannot possibly be denied that they have provided ways of life and contexts of meaning within which much of the rich and varied potential of human beings can be and has been realized (not least the reality of love and compassion). Within them too there has been a recognition of human finitude and openness to transcendence. More than that, from the perspective of Christian faith there is no difficulty in believing that the Spirit of God has been present and at work in these other traditions of faith, evoking and responding to the human quest for the ultimately real and holy.

In the second place, in terms of the argument proposed in this section, there is no reason to suppose that any religion or ideology anywhere has successfully escaped the pitfalls of idolatry or the tendency to mistake the medium or channels of grace for the source. The escalation of fanatical cults and fundamentalist movements provides all too much evidence of this tragic tendency today. One can therefore suggest that not only individuals, but all religions (including Christianity) stand in need of redemption, of liberation from self-created idols that stand between them and God, if they are to be brought or brought back into relationship with that which, or rather the one who, is ultimately real. If Jesus does in fact make possible such reconciliation, then he will be significant for all, though how that works out in practice for different people in different contexts and traditions cannot be anticipated (or dictated from outside).

We have seen how the traditional and problematic imagery of Christ's victory over the Devil might be reinterpreted in terms of liberation from alienation in a way that might resolve some of the problems posed by traditional imagery. We turn again now to an image of redemption that has always stood at the heart of both the worship and the teaching of the Church, namely, sacrifice.

Sacrifice for sin
The theme of sacrifice has already been considered at length in chapter 2, and so I will only comment on it briefly here.

Jesus' death can still be described as a 'sacrifice' in the traditional sense of an offering to God of a perfect victim whose blood serves to wipe out the sins of humankind. But it is here that difficulties arise. Why should blood sacrifice have been necessary? The appeal to scripture to justify it simply does not convince those who accept a critical approach to the Bible and recognize its historical conditioning. Even if the idea of a flawless victim is interpreted in profoundly moral and spiritual terms, the problem of the need for his sacrificial death is not resolved.

To repeat a point already made in the previous chapter, one solution is to turn the language round, or more precisely, to start with the user rather than with the referent of the word. Confronted with the fact of Jesus shameful death, witnesses to it faced a choice: was it punishment or sacrifice? Was it the death of one who deserved to die, a blasphemer or rebel rightly punished? Or was it a death acceptable to God, a sacrifice? To say that wouldn't explain anything so much as simply say everything. The implications were cataclysmic. If his death was acceptable to God, then his whole way of life which culminated in his death was acceptable to God.

The same point could be made in respect of other deaths, not least of the Maccabaean martyrs, but whereas they died for the Torah (and so reinforced its claims), Jesus, as we have seen, was amazingly independent of any existing cause. His death was God's cause in the sense that he died for the vision of God by which he lived. But his contemporaries had nothing else to go on to discover what that vision or cause was, other than Jesus himself, his person and life story and death. Hence to call Jesus' death a sacrifice was to declare him to be the revelation of God. In so far as in his life he had reached out to the fallen, the outcast, the sinner, and had challenged the power and authority of worldly and religious rulers, he revealed God to be against worldly power and domination and free to reach out to and raise up life's failures and villains, the marginalized and the dehumanized; he revealed God's freedom to affirm the humanity of human beings, however much that was lacking in the eyes of the world.

To see Jesus' death as a sacrifice, to respond to him as the place where God was seen and at work, had to mean more than merely theoretical assent. The question of God meant nothing if the answer did not imply ultimacy, total commitment – the whole history of Judaism from Abraham to the prophets to the Maccabaean martyrs witnessed to that. To call Jesus' death a sacrifice is thus to align oneself with his life, to deny the claim of any power or authority to exceed him, to be prepared to suffer the consequences as he did. It is at the same time to accept the affirmation of one's own humanity and the freedom and hope this brings, and to affirm the human worth of all one's fellow human beings. This cannot be merely a matter of words, but as in the case of Jesus, must be made real in actions – actions that cannot help but engender conflict wherever human value is denied, but which will help create truly *human* life wherever that goal is pursued.

It can at least be maintained that by focusing less on the word 'sacrifice' than on the one who uses that word, we escape many of the difficulties raised by an objectified external view of sacrifice – how it 'worked', why God insisted on 'it'. Our attention is concentrated instead on human response and decision, on the fundamental decision that confronts every person faced with the story of Jesus' life and death, whether to distance oneself from it, or to engage and be engaged with it and with all that it means and can mean. This is nothing other than the question of faith, and maybe it is only in faith that the mysterious final episode in the story of Jesus can begin to be grasped, the discovery of new life out of death, in short, resurrection.

Before exploring that theme in the next chapter, one more issue of fundamental importance needs to be addressed, namely, forgiveness.

The question of forgiveness

At the beginning of this theological exploration it was suggested that one reason for opposing doctrinal reconstruction was the fear of denying the reality of God in personal loving relationship. A criticism of the interpretation offered here might be that nothing is left of God outside the relationships of human beings to each other. One might reply that the freeing of human beings to become persons, and to be persons in loving relationship, might be not only God's way of working in history, but his way of meeting us in this world, not alongside but through relationships with other persons. If the doctrine of the Incarnation means that God was encountered in a human person, then to suggest that God is still at work in the bringing into being of truly human persons, and is to be encountered through our response to persons – our loving and forgiving – may not be as radical a reconstruction as it at first appeared.

Yet the objection may still be raised that human loving and forgiving is inevitably flawed. How can we be sure of unconditional love and forgiveness unless our relationship to God and God's relationship to us is something more than the mutuality of human relations? There is force in this objection, but far less in the obstacle often raised against God's freedom to forgive. The question 'how can we be sure that God forgives us?' is no different for those who stand in faith from the question 'how can we be sure Jesus forgives us?' Faith starts from the discovery and conviction that he does. Love is always free to forgive and to bear the pain of the offence that needs forgiveness. To forego one's rights in retrospect out of love for the offender is what forgiveness is, whether human or divine.

Too many theologians have imposed absurd limitations on God's freedom to forgive, as though God had problems which somehow Jesus did not face. But the love that forgives is on its own not enough to restore. Forgiveness has its own logic, it cannot be received by those who cannot or dare not recognize their offence. They need not only to see the truth about themselves but to accept the truth about themselves. That is not easy or even possible outside a relationship of trustworthy love, where the promise of restored relationship is given. It is only within such a relationship that the reality of sin emerges as something more deeply personal than the language of alienation and inauthentic existence can convey, however useful such language is in the analysis of the workings of sin. It is only where the promise of restored relationship – reconciliation, atonement – is given that we may dare to acknowledge the reality of sin. Thus faith sees in Jesus the true quality of human being, which itself discloses the truth about ourselves. But faith also receives from Jesus the promise of trustworthy love that makes it possible to accept that truth, however hard it is to bear, and so to be open to forgiveness. Where forgiveness is received, the stranglehold of the past is broken and a new future opens up.

But yet, the simple declaration of trustworthy love is not enough, and interpretations of Christ's atoning work which reduce it to such a declaration are inadequate, because the fruits of love and forgiveness cannot be fully enjoyed unless the power of sin is broken, whether it is at work in the individual or in society. The individual cannot be a person totally apart from society, and cannot be restored to wholeness apart from the restoration to wholeness of society. The reality of trustworthy love is itself confirmed through the gift of the power to defeat sin, in the individual and in the structures of society.

These pages have concentrated mainly on how we can recognize the reality of this gift and appropriate it in terms of our perceptions of our world today. Unless the Christian doctrine of the atonement can embrace the individual and society, and not only promise the reality of love and forgiveness, but show how the power to overcome sin and demonic forces is in principle available to us, it must be inadequate and unable to offer hope to the world we live in. But the Christian understanding of redemption does embrace the solidarity of human life, offer the power of transforming it, and give grounds for hope, however incomplete or inadequate this attempt to convey the fact may be.

So the life and cruel death of a Galilean holy man two thousand years ago is profoundly significant for our world today, which in terms of human conflict, frustration, fragmentation, guilt, and failure, may not after all be so very different from what it was in former times, however much our perceptions of the world outside ourselves may have changed. The next question is how we should understand the explosion of new life and hope that occurred in the aftermath of Jesus' death, and also how we can cope with the problems that poses for us today.

Notes
1 This chapter was originally published in *Religion of the Incarnation: Anglican essays in commemoration of* Lux Mundi, ed. R. Morgan (Bristol, 1989). It is published here with the kind permission of Continuum.
2 In *Lux Mundi: A series of studies in the religion of the Incarnation* (Oxford, 1889) 5th edn, p. 275.
3 For the use of myth in theology see Wiles 1977, 148–66.
4 Bultmann 1953, 1–44.
5 Heidegger 1978, vol. 2:1.
6 For a full treatment see Berger 1969.
7 Cf. Tillich 1978, i, 13, 'Idolatry is the elevation of a preliminary concern to ultimacy.'

4

THE TROUBLE WITH THE RESURRECTION[1]

No Christian theologian could ever rightly say that the New Testament was not his or her field. Those engaged in the task of trying to understand and to interpret Christian doctrine today must always engage not only with the text but with scholarly exegesis and interpretation of the New Testament, however troublesome that can be for those who would prefer to have sure and certain foundations on which to raise their doctrinal structures. This is especially true in relation to that central and yet utterly mysterious event described as the resurrection of Jesus, on which so much depends, but yet is so hard to fathom. The trouble with the resurrection is that while it is so fundamental to the Christian faith, it poses numerous problems.

These problems were brought into focus many years ago when there was a TV series *Jesus of Nazareth*. In a moving scene after the crucifixion, Jesus' almost naked body was laid in a tomb. But a few moments later he was shown seated in a room with his disciples. A little girl of seven or eight at the time at once asked, 'Where did he get his clothes from?!' I have not seen that particular point raised in print till recently by Paul Badham.[2] It's true that B.F. Westcott alludes to the question when he writes, 'A little reflection will show that the special outward forms in which the Lord was pleased to make himself known were no more necessarily connected with His glorified person than the robes which he wore',[3] but that simply evades the issue.

One might instinctively reply 'You're missing the point!' Maybe, but it's a perfectly fair question to put to those who uphold the empty tomb tradition and who, like Michael Ramsey, C.F.D. Moule and many others ascribe a spiritual body in some way continuous with his physical body to the risen Jesus. The idea of a spiritual body poses various familiar problems, such as how could it pass through locked doors yet eat fish, as Luke reports? What happened to the fish Jesus ate? More pointedly, what happened finally to the physical body Jesus died in and/or the spiritual body he rose in?[4] Christopher Rowland in the same volume seems to me to dodge the issue. He defends the empty tomb tradition and goes on to say, 'While not deterring the quest for answers to that kind of question, it seems to me that the New Testament indicates that our concerns ought to be primarily elsewhere.'[5] Of course! But those who do defend the empty tomb owe that little girl an answer. Without one, that tradition may be rather more open to question than Rowland appears to admit. Anyone advocating a strong version of physical resurrection certainly owes an answer. Stephen Davis argues for one of the strongest. He goes so far as to say that not only was the tomb empty, but that the risen Jesus had a body that was not only touchable but would have shown up on a photograph![6] To his credit, he addresses a great many of the problems and objections to his views, but rather surprisingly not the question of clothes.

I do not think it will really do for John Muddiman to make attack the best defence, when he writes 'Jesus' tomb belonged to Joseph of Arimathea and was discovered empty by Mary of Magdala. It is almost impossible to deny the truth of these two points. For if so, we would have to suppose not just the wish fulfilment born of devotion, but deliberate falsification backed up by the invention of two quite fictitious characters'.[7]

Davis even more strongly thinks that if there was no physical resurrection, then 'the first disciples were charlatans and dupes'.[8]

We need not think those are the only alternatives any more than we need think that the New Testament writers who used false names or invented stories were charlatans. To project our ideas of falsification to New Testament times would seem to be dangerously anachronistic. But if Muddiman's two points are to stand, where *did* Jesus get his clothes and what happened to them?

There are many other problems, which can be listed briefly, because they are familiar, and some of them at least may be open to solution. They come under two headings, biblical and doctrinal.

1. Biblical

Problem 1: On what day did the resurrection take place? Mark 8:31 reads 'The Son of Man must be killed, and after three days rise again'. That would suggest Monday. 'After three days' recurs on Jesus' lips again in Mark

9:31 and 10:33–34. Elsewhere as early as Paul in 1 Corinthians 15:4 we have 'on the third day', which is not quite the same thing; perhaps it reflects an attempt at harmonization, or more likely the influence of Hosea 6:2, 'After two days he will revive us; on the third day he will raise us up, that we may live before him'. (Interestingly the Septuagint reads not 'he will raise us' but 'we shall arise'.) But 'on the third day' only works if Friday counts as the first day. Both Luke and Matthew changed Mark's 'after three days' into 'on the third day' (Matthew 16:21; 17:23; 20:19; Lk. 9:22; 18:33; 24:7) Yet Matthew reverts to 'after three days' in Matthew 27:63. In fact the time between Jesus' death at 3.00 p.m. on Friday afternoon till dawn on Sunday was about thirty-nine hours, a little over a day and a half.

Problem 2: Where did the resurrection appearances take place? Mark hints at Galilee. Matthew puts the emphasis there with Jesus' climactic appearance on the mountain (Matthew 28:16–17). John 20 places them in Jerusalem, but John 21 sets the scene in Galilee. Luke firmly locates the appearances in Jerusalem. Paul tantalizingly does not say.

Problem 3: In relation to the Jerusalem empty tomb stories, how many angels featured? Paul of course has no tomb or angels. The Gospels differ over the number or time of angelic appearances. Mark has one young man dressed in white. Matthew has an earthquake and an angel descending from heaven, his arrival apparently witnessed by the women. Luke has two men in dazzling apparel; so does John, though they only appear and speak to Mary Magdalen after Peter and the other disciple have been and gone – the latter interestingly believed before any heavenly vision or appearance of Jesus.

Problem 4: How many women? Their names and numbers vary, though Mary Magdalen features in all the Gospel accounts (though not in Paul). Did they see the risen Lord in the garden? No, according to Mark, and also Luke, surprisingly, given his Jerusalem focus. Perhaps he wants to restore the disciples to pride of place despite their flight (Matthew 26:56). In Matthew, equally surprisingly, given his Galilean focus, the women do meet Jesus and are addressed by him near the tomb, though in a strangely superfluous way – just repeating the angel's message. In John, Jesus meets Mary Magdalen alone on her second visit.

Problem 5: It is a well-known fact that Paul does not mention any women at all in relation to appearances of Jesus, and adds other appearances not mentioned in the Gospels, and of course includes himself in the same sequence (see 1 Corinthians 15: 3–8).

Problem 6: I have already touched on the question of Jesus' spiritual body, which could apparently pass through locked doors. In which case why did the stone have to be moved from the entrance to the tomb, as reported in Mark, Luke, and John? Matthew offers a simple solution. The angel rolled away the stone in the women's presence to show that Jesus was not there, not to let him out. But just what is meant by 'spiritual body' and what sort of objectivity or physicality should be ascribed to it?

One might ask, if Caiaphas or Herod had been in the house opposite, could they have seen Jesus through the window in the upper room? We may well think not, if the appearance of the risen Lord and faith go together. Davis is at his weakest here. His suggestion that the risen Christ was photographable would seem to make his whole case suspect. Even Pannenberg accepts that the resurrection appearances were not visible to one and all,[9] but then what were they? What sort of reality did Jesus' spiritual body have?

Paul's familiar metaphor of the seed in 1 Corinthians 15 emphasizes the discontinuity between the seed that is sown and the body (blade) that rises from it. 'You do not sow the body that is to be, but a bare seed' (verse 37), 'It is sown a physical body, it is raised is a spiritual body' (verse 44). 'What I am saying, brothers and sisters, is this: flesh and blood cannot inherit the kingdom of God' (verse 50). Paul goes on to suggest a different metaphor of clothing, 'This perishable body must put on imperishability, and this mortal body must put on immortality' (verse 50). This only goes to show that metaphor and religious imagery should not be taken too literally.

Problem 7: Matthew poses a problem which we tend to evade. When Jesus was crucified there had been an earthquake, the rocks split and the graves opened, and, 'Many bodies of the saints who had fallen asleep were raised' (Matthew 27:51). If Matthew can say that, one might think that he would not have had much difficulty with Jesus' risen body. Yet to his credit, although he lets the women grasp Jesus' feet in the garden, his final portrayal of Jesus on the mountain in Galilee rises above any crude physicality.

Those are some but not all of the problems that arise from the Biblical accounts of the resurrection.[10] There are also doctrinal problems.

2. Doctrinal

Problem 1: The resurrection is commonly linked to recognition of Jesus as Lord and God. But why should it be?[11] It is sometimes argued that, Jesus' life having ended in apparent failure, God raised him from the dead to vindicate him in the face of all that had happened. But that would suggest that God saw that Jesus had failed in terms of his earthly human ministry and had one last desperate throw, one last super miracle to salvage the disaster, to prove that Jesus was the Messiah after all!

But this sort of *deus ex machina* is not a Christ-like *deus* at all. This argument postulates not merely an interventionist God, but an interventionist God of the worst kind, who achieves by *tour de force* what could not be achieved by Jesus as a truly human being, keeping faithfully to his vocation. In effect, it betrays his and our humanity.

Problem 2: The second problem with a physical resurrection is that it seems also to involve a miracle that looks like a conjuring trick (to echo David Jenkins, the former Bishop of Durham, but noting his disclaimer that he meant it was much more than that). Such a miracle can then all too often be appealed to so as to legitimate every kind of irrationalism and superstition, as if to say, 'If the miracle of resurrection is possible then any kind of miracle is possible'. There is then no need for critical reflection in the light of our present scientific understanding or of a profounder understanding of religious language as metaphor and symbol. Instead, the argument seems to be, if you can believe the resurrection you can believe anything – any miracle. This appears to be at the heart of N.T. Wright's argument.[12] Despite his protestations that the resurrection does not open the door to a miscellaneous appeal to the supernatural and despite his edifying words about the challenge of a new world-view grounded on the resurrection, he uses it to defend belief in a literal virginal conception. 'We can't satisfy post-enlightenment scepticism,' he writes, 'But in the light of the resurrection we are called to be sceptical about scepticism itself.'[13] Well, yes and no! Stephen Davis admits that two radically different worldviews are in conflict. So does Michael Ramsey,[14] but merely because both can be argued rationally does not mean that the one that accords most closely to a literal reading of the text has the best claim to be accepted.

Maybe if you can believe in the resurrection, you can believe anything; the trouble is that if you can't, you can't. The resurrection may indeed be fundamental to Christian faith and life, but a misrepresentation of it may be a fundamental and unnecessary obstacle to Christian faith and life. To suggest, as Michael Ramsey does, that 'if the evidence is pointing us towards a miracle, we will not be troubled' is to gloss too easily over real difficulties.[15]

Problem 3: A third doctrinal problem is that, taken as it stands, Jesus' resurrection to glory, especially if he is identified with the pre-existent Son and Second Person of the Trinity, can result in his sojourn on earth being regarded as an unpleasant interlude in his heavenly existence, necessary for him to do what he had to do to deal with sin and death, but now happily behind him. So his followers can share in his present glory, and justify the triumphalism that has tarnished the church for so long, as Leslie Houlden has remarked. He criticizes the common tendency (ever since Luke wrote his Gospel!) 'to see Jesus' resurrection as somehow cancelling his death and ensuring that the story has a happy ending'. He also criticizes 'that kind of attention to 'the risen Christ', as an independent object of devotion, which is the breeding ground of all manner of triumphalism, the nourisher of qualities the very reverse of those that mark the life of Jesus'.[16]

But are these problems real problems, or are we somehow missing the point because we have allowed ourselves to be misled by the Gospel accounts and by our historical methodology, as Peter Carnley intimates?[17]

It is widely accepted now that Mark 16:1–8 is the primary source for the story of the empty tomb, and that the discrepancies in Matthew and Luke are to be explained as kerygmatic and apologetic (that is, geared to preaching and defence) expansions of the Markan original.[18] Within these expansions one sees an increasing concretization of the risen Lord, in Luke especially. His motive may well have been anti-docetic (opposing the view that Jesus only *seemed* to be a truly human being of flesh and blood), but the result is to bring the risen Jesus back into worldly history[19] – not completely, as elements of the supernatural do of course remain in Luke's account, but too much. In effect, Luke's resurrection account re-historicizes Jesus with the result that he has to de-historicize him again with the ascension, an episode not needed in the other Gospels where Jesus' resurrection is left a mystery, as in Mark, or is much more closely tied to his exaltation, as in Matthew (and in a different way in John).

But Luke has set the trap into which historical critics fall by presenting the resurrection as if it were, even if only temporarily, an event in worldly history open to the methods of historical investigation. It is on that assumption that such questions as 'Was the tomb empty?' and 'What kind of body did he have?' and 'What happened to his clothes?' can be raised as the object of empirical enquiry, rather than in terms of what religious meaning might be derived from these accounts if they are viewed as symbolic vehicles of truth, as Robert Morgan suggests they should be.[20]

Insistence on the objective historical character of the resurrection traditions in Luke's day and in our own would seem to have at least one thing in common: a concern to emphasize the reality of the resurrection against any kind of docetism. That, as I suggest above, was almost certainly one of three factors at work in Luke's account, and it may indeed have served that purpose well. It does not follow that this is the only way or the right way by which the anti-docetic purpose can be served now. A second factor may have been a conscious or unconscious resort to the rapture motif which would be familiar to a Roman audience.

This is suggested by Edward Schillebeeckx and taken up by John Spong. To quote the latter,[21] 'In this model, when a pious or heroic person died, all of his or her earthly remains would disappear totally, because that person was believed to have been snatched up to heaven... (whence) this now divine life would regularly materialize', as 'recognizably human', 'especially to those carrying out the earthly work of the departed one'. In one Roman story the glorified Romulus revealed that Caesar was 'Lord of the world'. Thus Luke's counter-claim would be 'not Caesar but Jesus'. Spong concludes: 'In the service of this image Luke had to recast the resurrection tradition. It would never be the same after Luke had finished his work.'

A third factor can be illustrated with the analogy of the title 'Messiah' in the Caesarea Philippi episode.[22] Peter calls Jesus 'Messiah', and is blessed, according to Matthew 16:17. Peter then remonstrates over Jesus' talk of suffering and death and earns the incredibly violent rebuke 'Away with you, Satan (Go to hell!) You think as men think and not as God thinks!' In other words, Jesus seems to be saying 'You are right to call me Messiah if that means you respond to me as the agent of God's kingdom. But if so, you'll have to redefine Messiahship in terms of what I am and do. Don't try to force me into traditional messianic preconceptions about military victory and worldly triumphs.'

This serves or should serve as a warning to those over-inclined to think that the resurrection has to be understood strictly in terms of Jewish or Pharisaic preconceptions. Something obviously happened, and one of the best words to express it was 'resurrection', but it was not the only option. As often noted, the word 'resurrection' (*anastasis*) does not appear in the Epistle to the Hebrews. In Tillich's terms, the cross is event before it is symbol, the resurrection is symbol before it is event.[23] In other words, 'resurrection', like 'Messiah', is a symbol of Jewish hope. Like 'Messiah', when it is applied to the event of Jesus, it is both blessed and condemned. It can express the reality of hope fulfilled and life transformed better perhaps than any other word. It can also, like 'Messiah', intrude into that event undeconstructed concepts of hope and ideas about Jesus, and indeed preconceptions about God, which need radical reconstruction if we are not to go on thinking 'as men think'.

Indeed one of the worst troubles with the resurrection may be that it drags God back into undeconstructed human preconceptions at the

Chapter 4

very moment when, in and through Jesus, God was about to die to his old self and rise in Christ. I speak figuratively of course. What were to die were human misconceptions about Messiahship and therefore about God. Perhaps the former, Messiahship, did die and rise transformed as 'Christ', which amazingly quickly became the very name of Jesus within the Christian community. In the latter case, traditional ideas about God (and resurrection) were not allowed to 'die' or to be surrendered, and so did not have the chance to rise anew, transformed.

And Luke, I am suggesting, may have helped to contribute to this failure by not letting the concept of resurrection 'die' with Christ. He pushes the risen Lord back into Roman or Jewish preconceptions that have saddled the Church not just with the mystery that is proper, but with semi-superstitious or mythological ideas that are a barrier to the mission of the Christ and too big a concession to 'Satan' (to echo the extraordinarily tough language of Jesus' rebuke to Peter). Hence when Tom Wright affirms the church's belief that 'Jesus was the true and final revelation of the one true God of Jewish monotheism',[24] I can only say a very big 'yes' and an almost equally big 'no'. Marcion had a point though he put it badly.[25]

So I can only half agree with Christopher Rowland when he says 'I believe it is impossible to understand the resurrection in the New Testament without resorting to the future hope of Second Temple Judaism'. He continues, 'Early Christianity shared with the Pharisees a belief in the resurrection of the dead (Acts 23:6), but regarded this as fulfilled in the case of the Messiah, but awaiting completion for the rest of humanity.'[26] But if that fulfilment did not make all the difference, it should have done. If the early Christians could not escape far enough from their existing world-view, we can sympathize, but need not therefore tie ourselves to it.

Now Rowland may be right to say that the early Christians could have talked about exaltation without mentioning resurrection, but his examples of Enoch and Elijah are scarcely relevant. Unlike them, Jesus had just been killed publicly. Certainly he could hardly be exalted if he was still considered dead in every sense of the word. Hebrews fully recognizes Christ's death, and so his rising to life in some sense is indeed implicit in his Lordship, but not resurrection as portrayed in Luke, not a return to worldly history, let alone with an empty tomb.

It may be that resurrection talk arose as a seemingly natural consequence of exaltation talk, just as talk of an empty tomb was probably consequential on resurrection talk. Barnabas Lindars[27] and Anthony Harvey[28] make much the same point. Trouble comes when consequential talk takes on a life of its own, so to speak. Then we get what Lindars[29] and Tillich[30] call rationalizations and Leslie Houlden calls dispersal of belief.[31] We see a shift from 'God raised Jesus from the dead' to 'Jesus doing his own rising' and taking centre stage in a quasi-historical drama instead of being given centre place in the divine drama. As Spong writes, 'The importance of the tomb was no longer a sign that Jesus was reigning in heaven by the action of God, but a sign that the deceased person had come out of the tomb and was a walking, talking and eating person who was back in life as one who had been resuscitated.'[32] To add Spong's later comment, '[i]f resurrection cannot be believed except by assenting to fantastic descriptions in the Gospels, then Christianity is doomed!'[33] Possibly.

In contrast, Pannenberg asserts, '[i]f this [argument for the resurrection of Jesus] collapses, so does everything else which the Christian Faith acknowledges'.[34] And for good measure, to quote Westcott as quoted approvingly by Michael Ramsey, '[i]t is evident that if the claim to be a miraculous religion is essentially incredible, Apostolic Christianity is simply false'.[35] But perhaps Christianity can survive our ideas about it better than we imagine!

Turning to the insistence in our own day on the objective historical character of the resurrection traditions, this may well stem from anti-docetic concerns again, the fear that the only alternative is to surrender to the subjective vision or hallucination theories of Strauss and his followers. But to see this as the only alternative is perhaps to betray the fact that one is still in the Lukan trap, and offering the only alternative which would be acceptable to the historical critic on his or her own terms. This I think is what Francis Watson is getting at when he says that 'a revisionist interpretation of the event of the resurrection in terms of the disciples' experience of renewal has in effect rejected Markan reserve by locating this event within the general category of 'religious experience', thereby asserting its essential clarity and intelligibility to critical reason. But then it becomes a fundamentally different event to the one that is just beyond the bounds of the Markan narrative'.[36]

It might not be as alarming as some people seem to imagine if we suppose that human psychology was and is involved in relation to the resurrection. Nevertheless, what resurrection signifies may involve much more than mere subjectivism without having to be miraculously materialistic. A recurrent fault of so-called 'objectivists' is their assumption that God is on their side and that any supposedly subjective account is

Chapter 4

necessarily reductionist. But I do not see why a God who is thought to be able to act objectively in the most miraculous way is deemed to be unable to act subjectively, i.e. in human subjects, in a way that is miraculous but in a different mode.

Be that as it may, it is interesting that biblical critics have recently been suggesting not merely the priority of Mark's resurrection account and its expansion in the other Gospels, but also that the primary theme of the resurrection in the New Testament was the exaltation of Jesus to heaven, by the divine act of God, hence his vindication. Inevitably this was expressed, and one might say experienced, in terms of Jewish apocalyptic hope (to agree thus far with Rowland, but to question the controlling influence of Jewish apocalyptic). A return to the foundational theme of heavenly vindication may allow us to cast off or at least loosen the mooring lines that have tied the resurrection too closely to worldly history and so allowed too much legendary or mythical material to be attached to it and then to be taken too literally.

Schillebeeckx in fact argues that the most primitive strand in the New Testament (the speeches in Acts in particular) simply proclaim Jesus' vindication and hence his ultimacy in the face of victimization by the religious leaders.[37] The second primitive note presents Jesus as the passive subject of God's resurrecting action, which in Spong's words 'meant that resurrection was seen not as a resurrection back into life but as an exaltation of Jesus into God and God's heaven by God's divine action'.[38]

Barnabas Lindars argues that Mark 'preserves the sense that the resurrection is a theological statement about Jesus rather than an item in his life story'.[39] Francis Watson in his talk of Markan reserve goes on to say that

> [t]he manner of narration suggests an ultimacy which in Mark is left undefined, while in Matthew's narrative it eventually takes shape in the commission to make disciples of all nations, baptizing them in the name of Father, Son and Holy Spirit, and in the promise of the risen Jesus' eternal presence.[40]

Anthony Harvey is the strongest advocate of the view that heavenly vindication is the heart of the matter: 'The more profoundly one believed in Jesus, the more firmly one would believe that this vindication had taken place. No resurrection (*outside heaven*) [my emphasis] would be necessary.'[41] He reminds us that there is no mention of resurrection in Philippians 2 or Hebrews, and that it plays no part in the argument of Peter's sermon in Acts 3. 'No belief in the resurrection [into earthly life, one might add] is called for; only that the Christ, after his suffering, is now in heaven ready to return.'

The trouble with the Resurrection

Harvey suggests that 'resurrection' came to prominence because of the happy ambiguity of the word *anastasis*. It could convey the immediate personal experience of the witnesses that Jesus had returned to life, and also 'the faith of all his followers that...he had been vindicated by God and given a place in heaven'.[42]

This leaves us with three important questions to be considered:

Firstly, in the light of what has been said, are there any solutions to the problems posed earlier? Where did Jesus get his clothes? And can we say any more about how and why the Gospels were written as they have been written?

Secondly, what started it all off? What happened that had such a tremendous impact on Jesus' followers and exploded into a worldwide Church? Can we get anywhere near the source? Despite Morgan's counsel of caution that '[it] seems better to insist that how the disciples became convinced of God's vindication of Jesus is a secondary question which cannot be answered for sure'.[43] Can we answer it at all?

Thirdly, where and how do *we* stand in relation to that event?

To return to the biblical problems: both 'after three days' and 'on the third day' may be interpreted in conventional Jewish terms in accordance with the Scriptures (1 Corinthians 15:4) as a short period of time, which posed no problem until the empty tomb tradition established itself. Until then the location of the resurrection experience in Galilee could be accepted without any trouble, and its date left open. But that Peter and also Mary Magdalen were involved in an originating experience would seem hard to deny.

It may be hard to decide between different explanations of the empty tomb, if it is not historical, but the crucial point would be to see it as consequential to resurrection faith, and not its source or necessarily part and parcel of it, as James Dunn has rather unconvincingly argued.[44]

By consequential I mean that it might seem to have followed logically and inevitably from the gospel message 'Jesus lives', taken too simply in this worldly terms: 'If he has been raised to life then he cannot still be in a tomb'. Ps. 16:10 in the Septuagint could reinforce the idea that Jesus' body did not suffer corruption ('Neither wilt thou suffer thy holy one to see corruption', in contrast to the Hebrew 'For thou dost not...let thy godly one see the pit'). This psalm is quoted in Acts 13:35 and seemingly misquoted in Acts 2:31.

This logic might have facilitated the transfer of the resurrection scenario from Galilee to Jerusalem. Jesus died in Jerusalem and was buried there. So

Chapter 4

presumably his tomb, if he had a tomb, is there, and if he is alive, it must be empty. But where is it? By now nobody knows, but to contribute my own piece of speculation, perhaps Joseph of Aramathea offers his own *unused* tomb as a meeting place for a symbolic celebration, at Easter, or possibly more regularly on the first day of the week, very early, and with no worries that Sunday is only two days after Friday. Only later might one try to harmonize by changing the formula to 'on the third day'.

Carnley hesitates over the idea of a liturgy at the tomb, because this explanation has to overcome a natural Jewish revulsion from tombs as unclean places,[45] but this problem would not arise if, as I (very tentatively) suggest, an unused and so clean tomb was provided by the man who does feature in all the Gospel accounts. In any case, Lindars refers to Jewish evidence for tomb gatherings held outside the tomb of a loved one to show respect.[46]

The involvement of the women is another contentious issue. It is often argued that this must be historical because women's testimony was not valid in Jewish Law, so why invent such an embarrassing anomaly? As Hebblethwaite writes, this was 'a detail no one would invent in a culture which despised the testimony of women'.[47] But as Leslie Houlden comments,[48] the women's testimony is only an anomaly and therefore 'uninventable' if it is tied to an empty tomb event immediately after the crucifixion, not if the story of the women emerged in the later Christian community where women were held in high regard. In other words, Hebblethwaite's argument would only have force if one accepted the historicity of the resurrection event in Jerusalem two or three days after Jesus' crucifixion, when of course Jewish cultural conventions would still have prevailed. But we know from Paul's letters how quickly women came to play a leading role in the Christian community. Are we to think of it remaining so rigidly tied to the Jewish Law and custom at the later date when these stories may have emerged? On the basis of a later location of the resurrection event, we may more readily understand how Paul, although he makes no mention of women witnessing the resurrection, nevertheless helped to open the way for women to be included in the resurrection stories without embarrassment at the later date when the Gospels were written.

There is however much to suggest that women, Mary Magdalen in particular, were close to the original resurrection experience, which may explain further why they were accorded a significant role in the early Christian community. Their involvement in those later stories may also

The trouble with the Resurrection

have been felt necessary to fill the gap left by the fleeing disciples. Mark left them in flight, Matthew finds them in Galilee, Luke covers their shame and keeps them in Jerusalem, but by now the women are safely in the story and need not be excluded.

The very notion of burial is not as straightforward as it sounds. The allusion in 1 Corinthians 15 certainly does not imply that Paul knew of an empty tomb. 'Burial' might well be taken as simply confirming death. There is no instance in the Old or New Testaments where a dead person who has been buried is raised to life, apart from Lazarus, an exception that does indeed prove the rule. And as Spong notes,[49] there is the surprising passage in Acts 13:29 where Paul ascribes Jesus' burial to the rulers of Jerusalem who had him killed: 'They took him down from the gibbet and laid him in a tomb'. This does not quite fit the account given in Luke as well as in the other Gospels where Joseph of Aramathea takes the initiative for Jesus' burial, having opposed Jesus' crucifixion.

If we do locate the original Easter experience in Galilee, then there is a price to pay. The empty tomb, the angels, the women's visits, Thomas, the physical appearances and the clothes all follow the wise men, the shepherds and the angels out of actual history (but not out of the language of faith commitment). Was their inclusion in the first place a result of misguided speculation at best, or a gross act of falsification at worst? Spong finds a much more positive answer by attributing it all to midrash. N.T. Wright dismisses the idea out of hand, 'Spong has followed a blind alley to a dead end. The Gospels are not Midrash'.[50] Michael Ramsey at least allows the possibility of its use in Matthew. But even if the Gospels are not midrash, it does not follow that Spong was wrong about the creative input of the Gospel writers. If it is not midrash, what is it when Matthew attaches the journey to Egypt to Hos. 11:1, or when, as John Fenton argues, they engage in their different ways in answering the question, 'Where is Jesus now?'[51]

And finally, what did really happen? I will offer a very tentative answer, not with the conviction that it is right, but as a possible solution to some of my troubles. First, I assume that whatever resurrection is, it is revelation of the Lordship, that is, the ultimacy of Jesus Christ. Revelation is, as Tillich rightly said, two-sided, fact and reception.[52] For that reason alone Caiaphas would not have seen anything through the window, nor I suspect would we, because we have not been shaped in the same Jewish apocalyptic mould. And because we are all different anyway, no single account could do justice to the reality which can never be identical for

Chapter 4

any two people. As Peter Selby rightly argues, single accounts are ruled out.[53] Yet despite our diversity, we do also share a common milieu, and there may be ways of articulating the resurrection that can speak to us in community and not in isolation, especially as what we are as human beings is persons in relationship.

This then is my final suggestion. Jesus mysteriously broke the mould of existence, the inherited mould in which not only human beings, society, and religion, but even God, or at least ideas of God, had been shaped. Jesus lived and spoke for his vision of God and by doing so shattered the humanly constructed conceptual obstacles which barred humanity from God and hid God from humanity and concealed true human being from itself. In so doing he opened the floodgates for the divine Spirit to pour into the human spirit – into those at least who let themselves be broken open and allowed themselves to be filled with the divine. This was the experience made possible for those who acknowledged Jesus the Christ as exalted Lord. In other words, it could only make sense if Jesus' name, his very being was at one with the ultimate source of being. If that is true, then Jesus is involved in every resurrection experience. Resurrection is not just something in the life of his disciples. Jesus sharing the life of God is not left behind, dead and buried, even if his body is still in an unmarked grave. Even if he had been cremated, that, we may suppose, would have made no more difference for him than it will for us if our hope is to share in his eternal life, transcending space and time and the boundaries of physical existence.

This I suggest is far from subjectivism in the usual reductionist sense, when it is taken to refer to the natural response of some already existing human subject. Resurrection experience is conditional on a Good Friday experience, on the shattering of the subject, its death, before it could begin to experience the new possibilities of life. A shattering fact had to precede the transforming reception. If something like that happened to Peter and Mary Magdalen, and Paul, and many others at the time, perhaps it is not wholly removed from what can happen to human beings today.

The trouble with the resurrection is that we do not like having our moulds broken, or to put it another way, being stripped bare and being offered new clothes. What is undeniable is that the momentous event was bound up with the acknowledgement of the ultimacy of Jesus. In the next chapter I attempt to trace out the way or ways in which the early Church struggled with much toil and trouble and not always successfully to find the language that could do justice to their convictions.

Notes

1 This chapter was oriinally published in *Understanding, Studying and Reading: New Testament eassays in honour of John Ashton*, C. Rowland and C.H.T. Fletcher-Lois (eds.) 1998.

2 In Avis (ed.) 1993, 28.

3 Quoted by Ramsey1961, 47.

4 Cf. Badham in Avis (ed.) 1993, 28–9.

5 C. Rowland in Avis (ed.) 1993, 78.

6 Davis 1993, 24.

7 'I believe in the Resurrection of the Body', in Barton and Stanton (eds.) 1994, 131.

8 Davis 1993, 14.

9 Pannenberg 1968, 99: 'Because the life of the resurrected Lord involves the reality of a new creation, the resurrected Lord is in fact not perceptible as one object among others in the world.'

10 Such as the strange failure to recognise the resurrected Jesus. See Matt. 28:17, Luke 24:26, John 20:14

11 Hebblethwaite raises this question in 'The Resurrection and Incarnation', in Avis (ed.) 1993, 157.

12 Wright 1992, 82.

13 Ibid., 85.

14 Ramsey 1961, 56.

15 Ibid., 57.

16 Houlden 1986, 150–1.

17 Carnley 1987, 25.

18 Ibid., 46.

19 Ibid., 76.

20 R. Morgan, 'Flesh is precious: the significance of Luke 24:36–43', in Barton and Stanton (eds.) 1994, 18.

21 Spong 1994, 76–7. Cf. Schillerbeeckx 1979, 340–4. 'The 'rapture' motif eases the Greek conception of Christian resurrection.'

22 Carnley 1987, 53.

23 Tillich 1978, ii, 153.

24 Marcion seriously overstated the discontinuity between the God of the Old Testament and the God of the New Testament. See p. 47 n. 33.

25 The influential 2nd-century heretic who overstated the discontinuity between the God of the Old Testament and the God revealed in Christ and was condemned by the church. See Filoramo 1990, 164–6.

26 'Interpreting the Resurrection', in Avis (ed.) 1993, 70.

27 'The Resurrection and the empty tomb', in Avis (ed.) 1993, 129.

28 'They discussed among themselves what this 'Rising from the Dead' could mean (Mark 9:10)', in Barton and Stanton (eds.) 1994, 75.

29 Avis (ed.) 1993, 119.

Chapter 4

30 Tillich 1978, vol. 2, 127.
31 Avis (ed.) 1993, 61–2.
32 Spong 1994, 82.
33 Ibid., 238.
34 Pannenberg 1972, 97.
35 Ramsey 1961, 37.
36 '"He is not here": towards a theology of the empty tomb', in Barton and Stanton (eds.) 1994, 101.
37 Schillebeeckx 1979, 274, 278–80.
38 Spong 1994, 119.
39 P. Avis (ed.) 1993, 131.
40 Barton and Stanton (eds.) 1994, 104.
41 Ibid., 73.
42 Ibid., 77.
43 Ibid., 12.
44 Dunn 1985, 65–9.
45 Carnley 1987, 50.
46 Avis (ed.) 1993, 129.
47 Ibid., 158.
48 Houlden 1986, 147.
49 Spong 1994, 224.
50 Wright 1992, 73.
51 'The Four Gospels: four perspectives on the Resurrection', in Avis (ed.) 1993, 49.
52 Cf. Tillich 1978, ii, 97.
53 Quoted by Paul Avis in 'The Resurrection of Jesus: asking the right questions', in Avis (ed.) 1993, 7.

5

THE LORDSHIP OF CHRIST AND THE LANGUAGE OF ULTIMACY [1]

INTRODUCTION

The followers of Jesus discovered that somehow their own relationship with him was not broken by his death. A community came into being which found its identity in its commitment to him as the one in whom the truth of God was revealed, and in its conviction of his continuing living, personal healing presence. For those involved, this was somehow nothing less than the creative presence of God himself. Thus the two dimensions of personal knowing combined in Jesus, the objective knowledge of 'knowing about' which can be put into words, and the subjective knowing experienced in the intimacy of loving relationship, which can never be adequately put into words.

Because God himself was now seen in the light of Jesus, the significance of what was seen in him was bound to transcend the limits of Jesus' historical existence, without necessarily detracting in any way from his genuine humanity. From this it would follow that it is possible for the human Jesus to be the revelation of God without his life ceasing to be woven into the structures of evolution, history, and society. In other words, it can reasonably be argued that commitment to the man Jesus portrayed in the New Testament as the form (objective revelation) of God is the first and crucial step towards a right relationship with God. Within this relationship, Jesus' followers believe that the destructive tensions and distortions of human life are or can begin to be overcome, and the highest creative potentials of human beings may be realized, though not without struggle or pain.

Our immediate concern here is with the problems facing the Jesus-centred community in its attempts to communicate its convictions about him in terms that would do justice to what it believed and had received and

Chapter 5

wished to offer others. In short, how was faith in the ultimacy of Jesus to be understood and expressed? This will be the focal point of this chapter. The question cannot of course be divorced from consideration of the Holy Spirit, but its role will be addressed in relation to the Lordship of Jesus, rather than on equal terms such as a full treatment of the doctrine of the Trinity would require.

Paradoxically, the very thing that Christians wished to affirm, namely Jesus' continuing life-transforming spiritual presence, could serve to detract from the reality and significance of his historical life. Yet the conviction that Jesus' human life was real and important was too firmly embedded in the tradition to be relinquished, despite the intellectual problems this posed in relation to other claims that had to be made for Jesus. Part of the problem was that the very name 'Jesus' functioned ambiguously. On the one hand, it could signify the historical person in whom it was believed the truth of God was bodied out in history; on the other hand it could signify the risen Lord present in the spirit, and not easily distinguished from the Holy Spirit (as we find already in Paul, cf. Romans 8:9).

To put it differently, after his crucifixion, the concretely real, physical Jesus is no longer present in person as a revelatory point of reference for his disciples. Without that, competing claims to revelatory authority emerge, but the ensuing threat of anarchy is in due course fended off by the establishment of secondary points of reference, the canon of the New Testament and the authority of bishops. At the same time, however, it could be said that Jesus himself had moved off the stage of world history and had moved onto the spiritual stage, the realm of God's unbounded spiritual presence, but that stage is already occupied by the Holy Spirit.[2] To change the metaphor, it is almost as if we had two North poles (two *loci* of subjective knowing) and no South pole (no definitive objective revelation). In its absence, that space is all too likely to be filled by false and competing claims to ultimacy by the power hungry, but that cannot be pursued here. To return to the question of the Spirit, How can two North poles be postulated, let alone related to each other intelligibly? One or other would seem to be redundant and arguably this lies behind what has been described as the 'virtual binitarianism' of the early Church.[3] The problem could and did generate centuries of dispute.[4]

The questions of the relationship between the living Jesus (risen Lord) and the Holy Spirit, between the living Jesus and God the Father, and between the living Jesus and the historical Jesus who lived a genuine

The Lordship of Christ and the language of Ultimacy

human life on earth, still preoccupies Christians. The aim here is to explore the response to these issues as they emerged in the early church, and, in particular, to see how the language of ultimacy was applied to Jesus.

1. THE ULTIMACY OF JESUS AS THE REVELATION OF GOD

(a) The search for symbols

We must consider first what it was that Jesus' followers were attempting to do, and what their motives were. With the experience of Jesus' living presence came the conviction that he was indeed right with God, the true representation of God, and the agent of his purpose, and hence the key to a right understanding of God's relatedness to all human persons and the whole of creation – in short, the form of God. He could only be that in virtue of his perfect response to God. This could be expressed by designating him as Son (though that symbol was highly ambiguous and developed in a complex manner to be examined below). The conviction that Jesus was right with God meant that he not only revealed the truth of God, but the truth of human being in right relationship with God and thus as God had always intended. These convictions constituted the Christian Church. How Jesus could *be* that is the mystery of faith. How the conviction that *he* was *that* could be expressed is what concerns us here, together with the question of how the followers of Jesus could express their new identity in him.

Just as in the New Testament the language of ultimacy was transferred from the Torah to Jesus,[5] so the language to express the new identity that his followers found in him was drawn naturally for the most part from the language employed to express the old identity in the Torah.[6] Thus, the Jesus-centred community spoke of itself as the new Israel in contrast to the old Israel, bound to God in a new covenant, or new testament, in contrast to the old covenant. Other words took on new connotations, in particular *ecclesia*. Although used in the Septuagint for the assembly of God's people at the time of the Exodus, *ecclesia* had not previously acquired a clearly defined, technical meaning. It was now adopted by Jesus' followers as the name for the community centred on him, and in English is translated as 'Church'. However varied the forms and symbols in which the new community expressed itself, commitment to Jesus was the unifying factor of the Church as a whole, just as commitment to the Torah was the unifying factor within the diversity of Judaism.

Chapter 5

Not only was it necessary for members of the Church to articulate their own convictions to each other, but also to the world. If the truth of God and humanity was to be seen in Jesus, then he must be of universal and ultimate significance. So it would be necessary to find words that would serve the purpose of communicating this conviction not only in Palestine, but in the ever wider world into which the Church extended itself, where the value-laden symbols of Judaism would not necessarily have the same impact.

We begin with the task facing Jesus' earliest followers. Words and concepts to serve their purpose were already available within Judaism, and we must now explore them further. They may be roughly divided into two categories. On the one hand, there were those which signified the exalted status of human beings in the service of God, but who were necessarily distinct from God in virtue of their humanity (e.g. prophet, priest, Messiah, and also Son, though it could be used in different senses). On the other hand, there were the symbols of God's immanence – that is, of his outreach towards and activity within creation (e.g. word, wisdom, spirit, power). These two ways of thinking about God's relatedness converged in the attempt to interpret the significance of Jesus, and that convergence was the source not only of richly creative symbolism, but of acute tension in the history of his followers' attempts to speak about him. To appreciate the course the debate took, it is necessary to distinguish one further factor which affected the symbols of God's immanence.

Within the course of Jewish history an increasing sense of God's transcendence had emerged. But transcendence can mean different things. If the generalization can be permitted, it might be said that the Greeks were concerned with transcendent being, the Jews with the transcendent power. The transcendent perfect being of Greek thought was by definition utterly divorced from the realm of becoming. So it was logically necessary to postulate something to bridge the gap between being and becoming. There needed to be some distinct agent or metaphysical principle to mediate between the world of change and the remote, changeless, supreme perfect being of God. By contrast, in the mainstream of Jewish thought, God, though transcendent, was not remote. Even if as Creator he was wholly other than his creation, he was not excluded by definition from direct involvement in the scenes of worldly action. On the contrary, transcendent power could be expected to disclose itself in action, and Judaism was more concerned to affirm the reality of God's transcendent power, sovereignty, and purpose in the world (see Isaiah 40–55) than to ask how his divine essence stood in relation to material existence.

The Lordship of Christ and the language of Ultimacy

Accordingly, words and concepts were brought into service within Judaism to express God's active involvement in the world and in history, and his close relationship to humankind, without infringing his transcendence as properly understood. These terms, appropriately described[7] as 'bridge words', served in their original context as symbols of God's presence or direct agency, in contrast to the idea of 'bridge beings' as separate entities standing between God and the world. This distinction cannot be said to have been maintained unequivocally in early Judaism, but the exceptions prove the rule inasmuch as 'bridge beings' appear where the influence of Greek (and Persian) thought seems strongest. However, it is often not clear whether a term points to God in his immanence, or identifies a separate heavenly mediator, but perhaps such a clear-cut distinction was foreign to the author's own way of thinking.

Thus far we are presented with two broad categories of symbols: on the one hand those which express *God*'s direct or indirect outreach or immanence in the world and not separate realities; and on the other those which serve to identify *human agents* acting or destined to act on God's behalf, who in their humanity are clearly distinct from God. But the picture is not static. A widespread concern in the Graeco-Roman world to protect the absolute oneness of the supreme God led increasingly to the differentiation of the symbols of divine outreach into distinct spiritual realities or principles (sometimes hierarchically ordered). In short, 'bridge words' tended to become 'bridge beings', hovering uncertainly within a realm of existence between the transcendent God and the material world. Their ill-defined character would open up new possibilities and pose new problems for Christians as they moved into the wider world. On the one hand, clearly differentiated supernatural beings could more easily be identified with or at least closely associated with human agents; they at least had this in common, that they were other than the one Lord of Jewish worship. On the other hand, the lack of precise definition left open the question of just how distinct they were, or how close to God himself.

It was the various concepts and images which belonged to these different categories which were utilized by the followers of Jesus to convey the idea of his closeness to God and the belief that his activity in the world was on God's behalf. We must now return to these images, or the most important of them, first within the Jewish milieu and then in the wider Graeco-Roman world.

Chapter 5

(b) 'Messiah/Christ', 'Spirit', 'Lord'
The word 'Messiah' in Judaism had come to mean the divinely appointed agent who was expected to fulfill God's purposes and establish his kingdom, to whom therefore total commitment was due. No question as to the genuineness of his humanity need arise. Jesus was so designated, at least after his death if not before.[8] Applied to Jesus, 'Messiah' can be understood to symbolize his supreme status, but not his living presence. That could be symbolized by associating Jesus with Spirit (see John 14:17f.). The two terms, 'Messiah' and 'Spirit' could serve to identify Jesus as somehow at once the visible expression and living presence of God, This balance would not necessarily be disturbed by the representation of Messiah as a pre-existent heavenly reality, since as such, 'Messiah' was still exclusive in its application[9] – only one person could receive that title.[10] 'Messiah', whether viewed as a title or pre-existent being, could only have a single referent (unlike a more general term, such as 'prophet') If Jesus is Messiah, then the Messiah/Christ is indeed Jesus and no one else, which means that unlike the prophets he stands in a unique relation to God.

However, the exalted and exclusive connotations of 'Messiah' were weakened and almost lost when in its Greek form, 'Christos', it became simply a name for Jesus. Remarkably, this seems to have occurred as early as the writings of Paul. Perhaps it was the very strength of Paul's identification of Jesus as Messiah that rendered the title synonymous with the person (and hence in effect more nearly a proper name than was the case with 'Lord'; see below). The loss or at least the weakening of the historicality implied in the title 'Christ' may help to explain the one-sided emphasis on 'Christ in the Spirit' in Paul's writings, though the exclusive status implied in the title 'Christ' was still central to his message.

The word 'Spirit' on its own could express the creative outreach and living presence of God, but for that very reason could be wide ranging in its application (as in the case of the prophets); but without firm anchorage, the way to conflict was left open (as illustrated by the problem of false prophets). On the other hand, 'Messiah' unconnected with Spirit would be divorced from a sense of the living presence of God, which was unthinkable. However, linked with Spirit, the title 'Messiah' would provide the necessary anchorage and clear point of reference for objective knowledge of God, while the term Spirit could express the subjective immediacy of knowing in relationship. As complementary symbols of transcendence, Messiah and Spirit could not become entirely interchangeable. The seeds of trinitarian doctrine lie here.

The Lordship of Christ and the language of Ultimacy

In the non-Jewish world the title 'Lord', though ambiguous and open to a wide range of meaning, nevertheless could serve a purpose very similar to that of 'Messiah'. 'Lord' (Greek *kurios*) was used specifically of the Roman emperors, who were accorded divine status and who tolerated no opposition or competition. Hence, to proclaim '*Jesus* (not Caesar) is Lord' was to make an exalted and exclusive claim for him, and to risk martyrdom at the hands of emperors who recognized the political implications (especially when accompanied by refusal to sacrifice to the emperor or to the gods of Rome).[11] The use of the title for saviour figures in pagan mystery cults no doubt contributed to the religious significance of 'Lord', but for Christians it gained deeper meaning and its exclusiveness was reinforced when references to 'the Lord' in the Old Testament were taken to apply to Jesus. However, the word remained too ill-defined and widely used to serve as well as 'Messiah' could in identifying Jesus. It was for that reason, perhaps, that it had to remain one title among others.

To sum up, the close assimilation of 'Christ' with 'Spirit' in the language of the early Church effectively witnesses to the belief that the two aspects of God's relatedness with humanity are integrated in the one person of Jesus. He, then, is to be seen as both the source of true understanding and knowledge of God and also of a living personal relationship with him.[12] The Spirit informed by Jesus Christ the Lord and Jesus Christ the Lord experienced in the Spirit are indeed the one God known and experienced. Each of the two basic terms, 'Christ' and 'Spirit', carries a distinct meaning and hence performs a distinct conceptual function in disclosing God. Neither in isolation can adequately convey the reality of God in his relatedness. To treat them as interchangeable is to risk losing the content and force of each one.[13] Only in their dynamic interaction is God adequately disclosed.

The New Testament hardly represents the case exactly in these terms, but it may be for fundamental reasons of this kind rather than by chance that the contributors to the New Testament did not go further in rendering 'Christ the Lord' and 'Spirit of Christ' interchangeable, even when their immediate concern was with the living presence of Jesus. The power that flows from a generator may be one and the same and ready to flow out instantly wherever a connection is made, but the two wires cannot be reduced to one. No more can the poles of objective and subjective knowledge of God be reduced to one, and a wiring diagram that depicts the contrary is, to say the least, misleading and indeed, dangerous. Once the New Testament was formed, no theologian who acknowledged its

Chapter 5

authority could overlook the fact that within it Jesus was represented as Lord and Christ and as distinct from the Holy Spirit. This more than anything else was likely to hinder the identification of Jesus Christ with the Spirit, even though 'Spirit' had positive value already in the Greek world as a symbol of divine reality in relation to humanity.[14]

However, a problem remains. What has been said may shed some light on how the relationship between the Spirit and the historical Jesus might be understood, but the relationship between the Spirit and Jesus alive in the Spirit remains very unclear, because as such the Spirit cannot be completely identified with, or unequivocally differentiated from, the historical figure. At the same time, the combination of the symbols of man's transcendence and of God's immanence in the person of Jesus will inevitably pose a problem for understanding the being of Jesus, as to whether he was essentially man-transcendent, or God-immanent. Could he be both?

The question seems to have arisen at a very early date. The writer of the letters of John opposed those who appeared to hold that Jesus was God immanent as spirit, and only *seemed* to have a body of flesh (hence they are called 'docetics' from the Greek word *dokein* 'to seem').[15] On the other hand, the Ebionites, an early group of Jewish Christians,[16] held that Jesus was essentially man transcendent, a man inspired by God (cf. also Paul of Samosata). However, the debate would be pursued in somewhat different terms in later generations, where different symbols achieved currency. Their introduction can be associated both with the failure of 'Spirit' as a term with which to identify Jesus and with the fact that 'Christ' had become to all intents and purposes simply another name, while 'Lord' could still be used of God or man and so remained too ambiguous to serve the required purpose.

Where 'Christ' came simply to mean Jesus experienced as risen and living Lord and hence at one with God in his personal outreach to the world and humankind, a different word would have to be used to distinguish the historical figure, and, of course, the name 'Jesus' is available for this purpose. This leads to the contrast drawn in nineteenth and twentieth century theology between the Jesus of history and the Christ of faith, where 'Christ' has become synonymous with the presence and activity of Jesus in the spirit.[17] Paul could recognize the distinction but hardly the discontinuity often associated with the phrase.

At the same time, if 'Christ' seemed to be just another name for Jesus in the spirit, which appears to have been increasingly the case in the

Hellenistic world after Paul, then some term other than 'Christ' (and not 'Spirit' or 'Lord' on its own) would be needed to convey positively his high standing before God. This task presented itself in different terms from those which applied during or with reference to Jesus' historical life. At that stage 'Messiah' was the highest designation available for a human being. After the resurrection, the question concerned the relationship to God not just of an exceptional human being, but of someone apprehended as existing in the manner of God himself, in the spirit, with a claim to nothing less than the ultimacy of God. The right terms to define the relationship of Jesus in the spirit to God would then be those appropriate to spiritual reality, but not 'Spirit' itself. As remarked above (p. 90), other terms, such as Wisdom and Word, had already emerged within Judaism in the attempt to express the relatedness of the transcendent God to his world. As such they all carried more or less of the connotations of God in his outreach. This would render them highly appropriate to those who saw and experienced in Jesus the outreach of God. Such terms indeed were essential to express the conviction that Jesus truly and uniquely represented God, when neither the symbol 'Messiah' nor even 'Spirit' could suffice on their own.

At the same time, if God *was* definitively revealed in Jesus, it followed that God was not only like that then, but must always have been like that, and would always be like that (because God is eternal and unchanging in his nature, hence the alpha and omega). This would be so whether recognized to be so or not, and even when there could or can be no possibility of human acknowledgement, as at the beginning of the universe or the end. If it were not so, Jesus would not be the definitive revelation of God. (The aim here is not to prove that he was, but to examine the implications of confessing him to be so).

It follows from this that whatever symbols were used to portray God's creative activity, his all-embracing, providential care for creation and humankind, or the fulfilment of his purposes, these symbols must hereafter be tied to Jesus if they are to be apprehended and interpreted aright. If Jesus defines God, he defines the symbols of God. Conversely, tying such symbols to Jesus makes it possible to express what 'Messiah' partially but imperfectly expressed, namely, that *Jesus* is the true representation of God, the definition of God.

The traditional symbols of God's self-expression and outreach would serve this purpose effectively when linked to Jesus after the full force of 'Messiah' was weakened or lost. However, despite their positive value, these

Chapter 5

symbols of God's relatedness as applied to Jesus could also pose problems if they were treated as more than symbols, and rather as 'bridge beings' and personal agents of God's relatedness,[18] in some way distinct from God. Such a view might arise, as we have remarked, under the influence of Greek thought, but it would be reinforced, as Lampe suggests, by the complete identification of Jesus with such concepts.[19] Not only would they then impart to him a unique relationship to God of universal significance, but Jesus would impart to them the personal characteristics and differentiation from God which were his as a human being, and which constitute the fundamental conditions of personal existence in history. This will be explored below. The question will arise as to whether the differentiation that emerges between Father and Son is a fundamental condition of the being of God in eternity, as usually supposed in traditional understandings of the doctrine of the Trinity (in particular the immanent Trinity), or only pertains to God in his relatedness to humanity and creation (in short, the economic Trinity).

However, those issues cannot be considered yet. We must turn now to three symbols which were employed in the attempt to express Jesus' unique relationship to God, and hence his supreme revelatory significance, and which might thus serve to identify him as the object of ultimate commitment as effectively as the title 'Messiah' had done previously.

2. WISDOM, SON, AND LOGOS
(a) 'Wisdom' and 'Son'

The identification of Wisdom with the Torah (see note 5) may be reckoned to have played a key role in the elevation of the Torah to revelatory supremacy. It would play a similar role in the elevation of Jesus within Christianity.[20] As in the case of Spirit, the authority of use in the Old Testament scriptures could be claimed for Wisdom. In the key passage in Proverbs 8:22, and in many other passages where Wisdom appears in the Old Testament, it is very unlikely that there is any conception of a spiritual reality distinct from God.[21] However, in the book known as the Wisdom of Solomon, written in Greek probably not long before Jesus' day, Wisdom does appear more clearly delineated as a mediating figure. Not surprisingly, perhaps, the influence of Greek thought is generally acknowledged in this work. The Wisdom of Solomon and also the Wisdom of Ben Sira (Ecclesiasticus) were both included in the Septuagint (the Greek version of the Old Testament); and where it was used these later writings were accorded the same sacred authority as the rest of the Old Testament.

Thus, by the time of Jesus, 'Wisdom' was already established as a symbol of God's relatedness, and was perhaps already on the way to being conceived of as a bridge being, a spiritual mediator carrying out God's creative purposes.[22] Either way, in so far as Wisdom was associated with the divine plan for creation and believed to be the source of life-giving power, the image combined in dynamic personal terms the objective aspect of knowing about as well as the subjective intimacy of personal knowing in creative interaction. The emphasis fell more heavily on the objective side when Wisdom came to be identified with the Torah, so that the latter was seen as the embodiment or visible form of Wisdom. Such an identification said much for the Torah in associating it so closely with God and his purpose for creation. Equally, it said much that Jesus' followers wished to say about him in preference to the Torah, as the inspirational source of right understanding and right practice – the definitive clue to God's purpose in creation.

The letter to the Colossians draws the profoundest conclusions concerning Jesus' relationship to God through applying to him the imagery commonly associated with Wisdom, though not the word itself (Col. 1:15–20). Doubts over the authorship of this letter make it uncertain whether Paul's viewpoint is represented there. It seems very probable, however, that Paul was familiar with the Wisdom of Solomon. He was prepared, at least in opposition to contrary views such as seem to have been expressed at Corinth, to proclaim Christ rather than anyone or anything else to be the Wisdom of God (1 Cor. 1:20–5). In doing so, he was most probably 'asserting the finality of Christ's role in God's purposes for man and creation', to quote Dunn,[23] rather than intending 'to assert the pre-existence of Christ, or to affirm that Jesus was a divine being personally active in creation'. The connotation of pre-existence, or rather co-eternity with God, belonged naturally to the symbol of Wisdom. Its application to Jesus to express his ultimate significance opened the way to thinking of him as personally pre-existent.

Despite applying the image of Wisdom to Jesus, Paul more commonly speaks of him explicitly as 'Son' rather than 'Wisdom'. 'Son' had in the Jewish tradition long been used as a symbol of close relationship and service to God. It is hardly surprising that Paul preferred this personal symbol. It had, of course, the obvious advantage in Greek of being masculine, while 'Wisdom' (*Sophia*) was feminine.

The gender of Sophia would create no real difficulty where the word was used metaphorically, whether in the New Testament or in later writers.

However, if it was taken to designate a mediating figure, that figure would seem to be female. Outside the mainstream of Christian faith this could and did lead to the vivid mythological representation of the divine in terms of sexual differentiation, i.e. of God and a female offspring or consort. The philosophers and theologians of this period appear to have been strongly averse to this (not so the Gnostics and other popular religious teachers, which perhaps added to the word's disrepute).[24] As a result, ways of representing the divine in which both masculinity and femininity could be embraced were lost.

However, apart from such considerations, the feminine gender of Sophia hindered the identification of Wisdom with the man Jesus beyond the Pauline metaphorical level, and limited the possibility of personal identification with him. The attributes but not the name of Wisdom could be transferred to the person who perhaps even in his lifetime was called 'Son of God'. The result would be to transform the meaning of 'Son' as applied to Jesus. In his lifetime it could have been used of Jesus as of the Jewish charismatics[25] and other servants of God. But none of these was thought of as the Wisdom of God. To think of Jesus in the spirit as the Wisdom of God (as in Colossians), and still to call him 'Son', was to lift his sonship on to a totally different, supraworldly, suprahistorical plane. Wisdom elevated and conferred pre-existence on Son; Son differentiated and personalized Wisdom.[26] The two images in harness bore Jesus up to heaven and into eternity. More prosaically, in our terms, they served to express faith in the universal and ultimate significance of that human person, Jesus of Nazareth.

However, even in Paul's writings, 'Son' was not adequate in itself to define Jesus' relationship to God. In Jewish and Greek thought it remained full of ambiguities and potentially misleading connotations. A clearer designation was needed. The term 'Logos' seemed best suited for the purpose. It would itself in due course have its own misleading connotations corrected by the reapplication of the symbol 'Son', and would have its meaning enlarged by association with the imagery of Wisdom.

(b) 'Logos'

The Greek word *Logos* has no exact English equivalent. In everyday usage it can often be adequately translated as 'word', signifying 'the outward form by which the inward thought is expressed'.[27] But it might equally signify 'the inward thought itself', or both thought and expression together, or again 'reason', the rational principle underlying thought and speech. In

The Lordship of Christ and the language of Ultimacy

the period with which we are concerned, 'logos' had gained a wide range of meanings from its use in different philosophical and theological circles.

On the one hand, having been used in Greek versions of the Old Testament to translate the 'word' of God,[28] it could stand simply for 'God spoke' (see Jeremiah 1:4 'Now the word of the Lord came to me') or for the expression of God's power and purpose in creation, and so be closely associated with Spirit in the activity of the prophets. As such, it would scarcely be differentiated from God himself in his active outreach to the world. Hence, its meaning would be very close to that of 'Wisdom', its gender much to be preferred. On the other hand, it acquired significantly different connotations within the syncretistic philosophical movements commonly known as Middle Platonism,[29] which drew on the varied resources provided by Plato,[30] Aristotle,[31] the Stoics, and the Neopythagoreans.

Plato had distinguished between the worlds of being and becoming, the former immaterial and unchanging, accessible to the mind, the latter material and changing, accessible to the senses. In making this distinction he was wrestling with the problem of knowledge.[32] He asked how rational beings can know what is. This led him to explore the relation of universals to particulars. How, for example, is the concept or 'idea' of a table to be related to particular tables? The latter can be chopped up as firewood and disappear, But the 'idea' remains, non-physical in itself and immune to the processes of physical change and corruption, and, so it would seem, more real. Plato concluded that all things in the world, not only concrete objects, but concepts such as virtue and goodness,[33] are but pale fleeting copies of the immaterial, imperishable ideas, or forms. These he conceived of as not merely products of the human mind, but as existing in their own right in a realm more truly real than the only seemingly real physical world.[34]

Already posited in this account is the human being as knower, tied to the material world in virtue of his body, yet having access to the immaterial real world. This he had in virtue of his soul or mind. Although its destiny was to be embodied, and to impart energy and rational order to the body, its true home was in the immortal realm of imperishable being. Here philosophical and religious interests converge, and one can see how Plato came to exert such a powerful influence on the later history of philosophy and theology.

The function of the soul already described – to energize and order the body – and its intermediate place between the realms of being and becoming, would seem to have suggested to Plato a way of interpreting reality as a whole. In the *Timaeus*, he postulated as the organizing principle of the material universe a World Soul[35] – a sort of creator god which contemplated the world of forms and reproduced them as well as it could in the far from ideal conditions of material existence. Though Plato was not a fully systematic thinker and left many loose ends, he offered a comprehensive view of reality that was to have lasting influence.

Platonism did not, however, monopolize ancient thought. A different account of reality comes from the Stoics (who took their name from the *Stoa*, or porch, where their founder Zeno taught in Athens).[36] Although they posited two interacting principles, spirit and matter, unlike Plato, the Stoics taught that both were bodies, with spirit as a rarefied substance pervading the grosser material of the body, as the soul in a human being. In contrast to Plato's radical distinction between being and becoming, they portrayed the universe as a great ensouled animal, hence a living organism. Human souls were portions or sparks of the rational power governing the whole. This all-pervasive spirit of reason, the source of the harmonies of nature and of understanding in human minds, was called 'Logos'.

The Middle Platonists drew the Platonic and Stoic strands of thought together. The Logos and World Soul were equated, in some writers explicitly;[37] in others the idea of the Logos/World Soul is present, though the word 'Logos' is not used of it.[38] There remains one further contribution to the 'amalgam'[39] of Middle Platonism to be noted, which according to Dillon, imparted to it its distinctive quality. This came from Neopythagoreanism, with its 'postulation of a supreme, utterly transcendent First Principle, which is also termed 'God'.[40]

Plato himself had been much influenced by the early Pythagoreans – by their communal life, their fascination with numbers, and their 'mystical approach to the soul and its place in the material world'.[41] But here was something new. In combination with Aristotle's Unmoved Mover[42] and Plato's allusions to the idea (form) of the Good,[43] the Neopythagoreans contributed to Middle Platonism a profound sense of God's absolute transcendence.

Early Christian thinking developed in this milieu and could hardly have escaped its influence. In fact, there was much in the Middle Platonic vision of reality that was positively appealing to Christian ideas and interests. God was represented as supremely transcendent. In the perfection of his immutable being, he could not be implicated directly in the material world of becoming, but the spiritual world of forms (ideas) could be represented as existing in the mind of God,[44] as his inward thoughts prior to their expression in the creation – and the agent of expression was none other than the Logos, God's Word. Inasmuch as human beings, despite their material bodies, had a stake in the spiritual world in virtue of their reason (*logos*), the Logos (rational principle) could be seen to function appropriately not only as the agent of creation, but as the agent of reconciliation that would reunite estranged human reason with divine reason, humanity with God.

The Logos thus emerges as a key concept. It is the intermediary between God and the world. Like Wisdom, it is spiritual; but unlike Wisdom – at least in more orthodox Jewish thought – it is conceived in Middle Platonism to be distinct in being from the transcendent God, relating to him and expressing his mind and will, but relating also to the material world from which the pure essence of God was by definition excluded.[45] Yet, with that difference, the Logos in Middle Platonism plays a comparable role to that of the Spirit in Judaism, by signifying both the relatedness of God as far as that was possible in the immediacy of experience, and the world-creating and sustaining power of God. At the same time, as in the case of Wisdom, and more so than Spirit, the Logos represents the principle of order and harmony in creation.

With the Logos of Middle Platonism a concept became available of enormous value for Christians in their task of expressing the significance of Jesus. It was only to be expected that they would seize on it not merely as a vivid symbol of transcendence, but as signifying the true identity – the underlying reality – of that person who was called Logos in the Fourth Gospel and to whom, it was supposed, the Old Testament witnessed.

The question that now confronts us is the adequacy of the symbol 'Logos', seen against its Old Testament and Middle Platonic background, to express the ultimacy of Jesus. On the one hand, in the Old Testament sense, it served as a symbol of God's self-expression. Even allowing for some variation of usage, the less the differentiation of Logos from God, the greater was its value as a symbol of transcendence. On the other hand, as a spiritual reality distinct from the supreme God in the Middle Platonic sense, 'Logos' could more readily than 'Spirit' lend itself to complete identification with Jesus as a spiritual being distinct from the God whom, in his earthly life, he had addressed as 'Father'.

With these advantages Logos nevertheless introduced into Christian thought a complementary set of disadvantages. These sprang, first, from the limitations of the Old Testament meaning of 'Logos' as a symbol of Jesus; secondly, from the limitations of the Middle Platonic sense of 'Logos' as a symbol for Jesus; and thirdly, from the complications created

Chapter 5

by the application of 'Logos' in both senses to Jesus, and their interaction with other symbols of transcendence applied to him.

In the first case, to call Jesus 'Logos' in the Old Testament sense served well to convey the conviction that in him the truth of God was expressed. 'Logos' in this sense could function as a vivid metaphor like 'Wisdom', and in this context had connotations not merely of verbal expression, but of active power, very close to 'Spirit'. Indeed the early fathers were often unclear whether it was the Word or Spirit which inspired the prophets. Either way, the inspirer was God, and in this role the Logos was virtually a synonym for God. So to call Jesus the Logos was to call him God. This suited Christian purposes very well except that in this framework, the Logos so understood as the Word of God could scarcely be conceived of as a separate being, able to enter into a personal relationship with God as Father (which the New Testament demanded). In short, it would seem that Jesus the Logos could be God, but not quite real in himself as a distinct being, or else he could be real, but not quite God, if the scandal of two gods was to be avoided; worse still, if the Logos was 'real' in itself, the problem would return not only as to how the Logos could relate to God the Father, but how it could relate to the real historical person, Jesus of Nazareth (issues to be explored further below).

In contrast, the Middle Platonic conception of hierarchies of being meant that the Logos was not only distinguished from, but necessarily set below, the supreme God. It could be associated with the world of becoming, with history, concrete existence, and manifestations in material form, from which God in his perfect being was by definition excluded. But that he was so superior, separate, and inaccessible was not what Christians ultimately wished to say about God the Father. Moreover, though 'Logos' in this sense allowed them to say much that they wanted to say about Jesus, ultimately it did not say enough.

The problems would have to be faced in due course, but it can hardly be doubted that, in the first instance, 'Logos' was the most powerful symbol available to convey to a non-Jewish world the closeness of Jesus' relationship to God, and the conviction that in him the form and vitality of God were expressed in the sphere of creation. The disadvantage of the distinction of the Logos from God could to some extent be qualified by emphasizing the basic (and Stoic) meaning of 'Logos' as thought in the mind prior to outward expression.

Thus, the early Christian Apologists, such as Justin Martyr and Tertullian, could argue that the Logos originated within but became differentiated from the Father.[46] On this understanding, Jesus as the Logos could be thought of as standing as close to the mind and being of the Father as possible. (The actual designation of God as 'Father' was not unfamiliar to Greek ears, though it had the connotation 'Father of the Universe' rather than 'Father of the Logos as Son'.) 'Logos' also shared with 'Spirit' the authority of scriptural usage, but had a further advantage. In the Fourth Gospel the Logos was already explicitly identified with Jesus, in distinction from the Spirit. Whatever uncertainties still remain concerning the precise meaning of 'Logos' in that Gospel compared with later usage, and however hard it may be in practice to perceive clear distinctions in meaning between 'Logos', 'risen Lord', and 'Spirit', the logical problem posed by identifying Jesus with Spirit, from which he is explicitly distinguished in the sacred and authoritative writings, would not arise in the case of Logos.

The term Logos had also already been developed in the sphere of Judaism by Philo of Alexandria as a way of linking the Old Testament to Platonism.[47] In the process, he came very close indeed to transforming 'Logos' from a bridge word into a bridge being (without apparently seeing any great problem in doing so). Philo's influence within Judaism was not great, but by linking the Old Testament 'Word of God' with the 'Logos' of Middle Platonism, he served the interests of Christian theologians very well. Aided by Philo, they could attribute what was said of the undifferentiated word of God himself in the Old Testament to the differentiated Logos of Middle Platonism as identified with Jesus. Meanings never originally intended could then be read into scripture, more or less unconsciously. In other words, as we have seen, Christians could treat references to the 'Word of God' as references to Jesus the Logos; just as references to the 'Lord' in the Old Testament had been taken as references to the Lord Jesus.

However, it is here that we see the source of further difficulties. The use of the one word 'Logos', which served to unite Jewish and Greek ideas of transcendence in Jesus, could also serve to conceal serious underlying differences of interpretation. The semblance of agreement would be shattered when different ways of understanding Jesus and his significance developed according to different presuppositions over the meaning of 'Logos', and matching differences would emerge concerning his redemptive work. Out of this would arise violent controversies concerning the relationship of the Logos to God the Father on the one hand, and on the other its relationship to Jesus the man. The former issue came to a head in the Arian dispute, which will concern us in the following section. The latter gave rise to the Christological controversies between the Platonically-minded theologians of Alexandria in Egypt and the more traditionalist, biblically-minded theologians of Antioch in Syria;[48] these will be considered in section 4 below. All parties would be challenged not only by their direct opponents, but by the tension generated between the connotations of their own understanding of the Logos-symbol and what the faith and worship of the Church required to be said of Jesus who was identified with the Logos.

3. THE LOGOS AS JESUS IN RELATION TO GOD

'Thou art the Logos!' I have tried to show how the symbol 'Logos' in a manner analogous to 'Messiah' in the Jewish world, could serve better than any other symbol available in the Greek world at the time to convey Jesus' unique standing in relation to God, and hence his unique ultimate authority and revelatory significance. Other well-established symbols of transcendence or divine outreach, such as 'Spirit' or 'Wisdom', could not, for reasons already discussed, be applied exclusively or without qualification to Jesus, though they might be used metaphorically. 'Logos', however, seemed free of such limitations and so capable of being applied not merely metaphorically but literally to Jesus. In so far as Jesus was identified with the Logos, the Logos could serve to identify Jesus (to establish who he was), to disclose his relationship to God and hence to everything else. Its importance within the Christian tradition is that, even when the term 'Logos', and the way of thinking associated with it, fell more or less into disuse, it had already done its work laying down the terms for talking about Jesus and God. It had, perhaps more than any other word, fixed the rules for theological play, rules which it seems can still hardly be questioned without provoking indignant protest.

However, we have already seen that the symbol 'Logos' itself is of mixed parentage, and this alone makes it hard to see what applying it literally to Jesus should mean, quite apart from the problem raised by any attempt to speak of the things of God literally. Such difficulties were not long in making themselves felt in the early Church.

The relation of the Logos to the Holy Spirit did not receive close attention till late in the fourth century, and will not be pursued further here except for a brief indication as to why this was so. Once Jesus was identified with the Logos, the tendency we noticed before in the New Testament to assimilate him to the Spirit was checked. Yet their roles seemed to be interchangeable in the early years of the Church. Grillmeier maintains that ways of speaking about Jesus which relate him to Spirit or Logos, to be found in certain early theologians, are 'identical in point of content of ideas'.[49] If

The Lordship of Christ and the language of Ultimacy

'Logos' embraces the meaning of 'Spirit', the latter would seem to be superfluous, or else simply another name for the same thing.

However, in the New Testament (by this time recognized as sacred revelation), and also in traditional rites such as baptism, Jesus and the Holy Spirit were both named separately in relation to God. The apparent identity of content and distinction of beings would have significant consequences in due course. Before turning to them, we must pursue the problems that arose specifically over the relationship of the *Logos as Jesus* to God, and over the relationship of the *Logos as God* to the historical figure Jesus. The problem shaped itself differently according to whether Old Testament or Middle Platonic connotations of 'Logos' predominated, and was further complicated by the fact that the different points of view interacted on each other.[50]

The Old Testament sense of 'Logos' was originally predominant among those who stood in the theological tradition of Antioch. Its advantage was that it signified God expressing himself. So if Jesus was Logos in this sense, it meant he really was God's direct self-expression. This Logos, however, could hardly be differentiated from God in any real way, least of all in terms of the personal relationship which the Gospels portrayed between Jesus and the Father. Those who set great store by that relationship and by the whole of Jesus' earthly life, as the Antiochenes did, would therefore find it virtually impossible to identify Jesus completely with the Logos. However close a relationship might otherwise be asserted, some sort of gap between the divine changeless Logos and the truly human Jesus would have to be kept. Yet without their identification the ultimacy, and so the supreme revelatory significance of Jesus, could seem in doubt. The 'gap' would mean that the ultimacy ascribed to the Logos embodied couldn't easily be carried over to the man embodying it.

The understanding of Logos as derived from Middle Platonism was more characteristic of Alexandrian theology (though not of all Alexandrian theologians). We have already noted above some of its advantages and disadvantages. Logos in this sense, distinct from God the Father, could more easily be fully identified with Jesus and so help to maintain his distinction from the Father. But it could only do this at the price of setting him on a lower plane. Once again his ultimacy could seem to be in doubt.

The identification of Jesus with the Logos posed a two-sided problem. The Logos distinct from God must either be equal to God or inferior. If he was equal, there would appear to be two Gods; but to postulate two first

Chapter 5

causes was absurd, and in any case Christians had died for their rejection of polytheism. There seemed to be two logically possible alternatives. One was to suppose that Jesus and God (the Son and the Father) were the same thing (this view, known as the Sabellian heresy, was condemned on scriptural grounds). The alternative was to maintain that only God the Father was truly God; the Logos was not only distinct but inferior (the view condemned in due course as the Arian heresy – see below). If the Logos was inferior to God (and so in some sense a creature), then, as noted above, he could more readily be identified with the Jesus who experienced the various limitations of life on earth; at the same time the problem of two gods was avoided. But if Jesus was the Logos who was not quite God, how could he be worthy of worship? Was worship of him idolatrous? Yet Christians had died for refusing to abandon worship of Jesus the Messiah. Somehow he was entitled to more than the Logos from this perspective could give.

Thus, whether from the biblical or Platonic point of view, the problems posed by the identification of Jesus with the Logos were acute. Any kind of identification would strike non-Christian thinkers, Jew and pagan alike, as absurd. Jews could hardly tolerate the personification of the word of the Lord. For Middle Platonists, the assertion that the Logos was immanent in the world was one thing: to say that he was fully present, or worse, enfleshed (incarnate), in one particular human being was very much another – literally non-sense.

The early Christian theologians inevitably shared many of the philosophical and theological presuppositions of their critics, and so would have felt the force of their objections. They were faced with the task of making sense to themselves, as well as to others, of what the Church claimed about Jesus. In pursuing this task, they were working with symbols and ideas which were not only more or less the common stock of their world, but had also already been worked over, stretched, and refashioned within their own tradition. In this continuous dynamic process, many factors were at work.[51] Not the least significant was the interplay of symbols on each other resulting from their common application to Jesus, as we saw in the case of 'Wisdom' and 'Son'. This interplay can be seen to embrace 'Logos' as well, and to extend between the two senses of 'Logos', with both positive and negative consequences. The different configurations can be briefly described.

The subordinationist implications of the Middle Platonic Logos could be compensated for in two ways. On the one hand it could be combined

The Lordship of Christ and the language of Ultimacy

with or set alongside Logos language drawn from the Old Testament. On the other, the gap could be closed or at least narrowed by transferring the symbol 'Son' to the Logos.

In the first case, the undifferentiated Logos (word of God in the Old Testament) could serve to counterbalance the over-differentiated Logos (World Soul of Platonism). Both Logos symbols could serve in their different ways to convey the revelatory significance of Jesus; used together they would affirm him to be one with and yet distinct from the Father. As an expression of the paradox of faith calling for further reflection, this could serve a useful purpose. However, where such language was thought to describe who and what Jesus was, the use of the single term 'Logos' concealed rather than resolved the logical difficulties and obscured the paradox. A likely consequence was over-confidence in the language used, and an unsympathetic hostility towards those who would not gloss over the underlying problems.

In the second case, the symbol 'Son' could serve to draw the Logos into a 'natural relationship' relationship with the Father, (as against adoption), and hence on to the same plane as the Father. But 'Son' affected 'Logos' in more than one way. In the first place, it personified the metaphysical concept of Logos (in similar fashion to Wisdom) and placed it within a personal relationship to the Father. In so doing, it helped to displace the Platonic connotations of God's fatherhood in Christian theology, so that (as noted above) God the Father of the Universe gave way to God as Father of the pre-existent Logos-Son. More than this, 'Son' was also the channel through which the connotations of Wisdom could flow freely into 'Logos', and so strengthen its link with Old Testament usage.

The interplay of Son and Wisdom began, as we have seen, at least as early as Paul. Their combination would serve to express the ultimacy of Jesus which in traditional terms meant raising Jesus on to the same level as the Father. The Son metaphor in the Old Testament sense could not have achieved this on its own. Traditionally 'Son' could be used of kings or holy men or anyone in close, obedient and loving relationship with God. It never implied natural biological kinship, but rather adoption. The biological aspect of the metaphor, however, played an increasingly important part in later Christian discussion, where the precise relationship, not of the historical Jesus, but of the Logos-Son with the Father, was at issue.[52] Then the combination of 'Son by nature' with Wisdom imagery served effectively to elevate the Middle Platonic Logos on to the same plane as the Father, and so into equality with him. By this means, conceptual thought could catch up with the demands of faith, which insisted that Jesus was a worthy object of worship and therefore not less than God. Yet, though the imagery could serve this purpose, it was still more an expression of faith than an explanation. The mystery of the relationship between Father and Son, and the problem of the ultimate oneness of God, remained unresolved.

The symbol 'Son' functioned in a contrasting way when conjoined to Logos where the Biblical sense of 'Logos' was dominant, as in the Antiochene tradition. Here 'Son' served to differentiate rather than to elevate the Logos. The Word of God, which in the Old Testament was the expressive power of God directly at work, as in the prophets, became as Son a mediating personal agent, not identical with God the Father (neither was it identical with the human Jesus; this raised problems which will be considered in the next section).

The same word, then, could mean very different things, and the same symbol could function in contrasting ways according to the particular context of theological discussion. It is not surprising that disputes were often fuelled by widespread misunderstandings.[53] These disputes may be reckoned to fall into two basic categories. On the one hand, there were those where different language and different traditions of thought raised the often mutual suspicion in different quarters that the ultimate and universal significance of Jesus was being put in question by those who professed to be Christians. Where that was not the intention or the implication recognized by those accused, the issue could in the end often be resolved, even if bitter hostility and mutual excommunication marked the route. The qualifying of symbols and balancing of statements as described above would have their place in disputes of this kind, and open the way to mutual recognition.

On the other hand, there were disputes where, in our terms, the heart of the matter was whether Jesus really was of universal and ultimate significance or not, in short, whether he was God. We must here recognize that, whatever else it means, the word 'God' itself functions as the supreme symbol of ultimate and universal significance. As a symbol, it was open to the same dynamic interplay as the other symbols we have discussed. However difficult it might be to fathom its meaning and proper application, failure in the last resort to designate Jesus as God would entail the denial of his universal and ultimate significance, and hence the betrayal of the conviction on which the Church was founded. However significant Jesus was otherwise deemed to be, to call him less than God was to say

The Lordship of Christ and the language of Ultimacy

too little. If Jesus was believed to be the Logos-Son, then equally the Logos-Son must be called 'God', even if such a claim raised insuperable intellectual problems. A further distinction may be drawn between those who believed that salvation depended upon a unity of being between Son and Father (ontological union) or on a unity of will (moral union). The difficulty of embracing both aspects was and remains acute.

These, we may hold, were the issues at stake in what was perhaps the most bitter controversy in the early Church, the Arian dispute. Arius was a presbyter of Alexandria, and heir to the traditional identification of Jesus with the Logos. But he qualified that identification, and distinguished between the Logos which was eternally in God as his immanent reason, and a 'certain one'[54] whom God created to be his agent in creation and redemption, who could be called 'Logos' or 'Son' by courtesy rather than by right.[55] By identifying Jesus with this Logos-Son, Arius acknowledged him to be supreme over all creation and uniquely close to the transcendent God. Only someone within the circle of Christianity could make such an exalted claim for Jesus. Nevertheless, Arius was ready to accept the implication discussed above that Jesus as Logos-Son was less than and indeed wholly other than God. Arius broke out of the concealed ambiguities of the Logos-tradition by refusing to resort to the counterbalancing 'Word of God' language of the Old Testament. On his terms it could not be used in that way. In opposition to current trends, he re-emphasized the biblical idea of sonship, as implying a moral relationship of love and obedience rather than natural kinship. Jesus the Logos was adopted Son rather than Son by nature.[56]

Arius' solution had two great advantages. He was able to avoid the problem of having to show how the Logos-Son could be God without there being two Gods, or the one God being divided or changing, and he certainly had no truck with the Sabellian idea of Father and Son being one thing. Secondly, his Logos-Son, as a creaturely being, was logically free to conform to or not to conform to God's will. His actual love and obedience were therefore morally authentic, and not of necessity. Arius could thus do justice to the New Testament account of Jesus' experience of temptation and suffering, something which the defenders of Jesus as the incarnate divine Logos-Son were hard pressed to explain.

It remains the case that Arius' Jesus was not really human like us, because the pre-existent Logos, even if not God, was nevertheless far above humanity and in Jesus displaced his human soul or rationality. This aspect of Arius' teaching left a surprising number of his Alexandrian contemporaries undisturbed, including his famous opponent Athanasius (but, interestingly, not Eustathius, Bishop of Antioch). But perhaps the lack of criticism at this point is not so very surprising, since Arius' Logos was at least like us in being a rational creature, and in his creaturely freedom was able to achieve through his obedience to God a genuine moral victory over sin. By thus showing other rational creatures the way, he could secure their salvation. It has been argued that Arius' primary concern was indeed soteriological rather than philosophical[57] or merely the result of his anxiety to protect the transcendent oneness of God.

Whatever his main concern may have been, Arius' solution won considerable but not unanimous support. The protracted controversy he set in motion divided the Church just when the newly emerged sponsor of Christianity, the Roman emperor Constantine, was looking to it to help unite the empire. Constantine summoned a general council of the Church in AD 325 at Nicaea (by the Sea of Marmora, in what is now Turkey). Among those who attended were Bishop Alexander of Alexandria and his deacon, Athanasius, who would soon after succeed Alexander as bishop. It was not long since the Church had been subjected to severe persecution by Constantine's predecessors. For the 220 bishops assembled at Nicaea[58] to be received with great honour by an emperor, who refused even to take his seat before them, would have been an awesome experience.[59] It would also make it very hard for them to oppose his wishes.

A creed was approved at the Council which all the bishops present were required to sign. A word had been introduced into it, possibly at the emperor's own suggestion, which was designed to exclude Arius' viewpoint. The Greek word, *homoousios*,[60] meaning 'of the same substance', was not scriptural and was therefore suspect to many, but it seemed to be the best term available to establish Jesus the Logos-Son's position on the side of God rather than of creation, as Son by nature rather than by adoption. It scarcely explained how the two, Father and Son, could be one God, and it was open to different interpretations, but at least it appeared to establish Jesus' ultmacy, his worship-worthiness as God. Arius' own teaching was explicitly condemned. All the bishops signed the creed except two (and their motives were not, it seems, primarily theological).

But the Council did not succeed in unifying the Church. The controversy broke out with even greater intensity and lasted for many more decades.[61] Somewhat surprisingly, the keyword *homoousios* was at first more or less ignored even by supporters of the Nicene position, till Athanasius in particular re-employed it to maintain the full divinity of the Son against the later Arians. His cause finally triumphed at the Council of Constantinople in AD 381. It is the Creed believed to have been promulgated there which is still used in most Christian Churches and called the Nicene Creed. It differs from the original creed of Nicaea in having an expanded section on the Holy Spirit. Otherwise its significance lies in its reaffirmation of *homoousios* and so of the Son's full divinity. The Council marked the virtual end of Arianism, except on the borders of the Roman Empire.

For all the complexities of the debate, the clash of personalities and the interference of emperors, the conclusion of the dispute with the defeat of Arianism ought not to be regarded as a historical accident which might easily have gone the other way. The logic of Christian commitment required otherwise; the defeat of Arianism was inevitable, if the Christian Church was not to surrender the central conviction by which it was constituted. Arianism could do more justice than many of its opponents to the moral character of Jesus' life, but it failed to do justice to the conviction, witnessed to in the New Testament and upheld by the earliest Christians, that Jesus was of ultimate significance. Arius' failure to maintain the absolute uniqueness of Jesus' sonship in principle is precisely the point at which the inadequacy of his account emerges.[62] In our terms, Jesus, as represented by Arius, was not incontrovertibly the form of God.

One must add, however, that on Arius' own account Jesus came nearer to being that than anything or anyone else had been or ever, perhaps, could be. His intentions in faith may well have been more adequate than the language he employed to express them. Unfortunately, in that age, inadequacy of language was almost universally assumed to represent inadequacy of faith, if not sheer perversity. But at the end of the day, for Jesus to be above creation but below God, as Arius suggested, was not good enough for the worshipping church.[63]

It is of particular interest here to note that in order to make the point that needed to be made, the Church was driven beyond the symbols of transcendence derived from scripture. The language of philosophy had already been harnessed alongside biblical language in the task of apologetic and teaching about God, but, before Nicaea, no blatantly philosophical, non-scriptural terms had been incorporated into the central confessions of the Christian faith. We have already noted the suspicion which the term *homoousios* aroused on this account. Yet the expression 'of the same substance as the Father' (or 'one in being with the Father') had to take its place alongside 'Son' if the ambiguities of traditional symbols were to be overcome and the ultimacy of Jesus maintained. The Arian controversy, like

Chapter 5

many other theological conflicts, is a witness to conceptuality struggling painfully to catch up with commitment.

The language of 'substance', 'nature', and 'person' was to acquire increasing significance from now on. But though such terms might counter the ambiguities of traditional symbols, they introduced new sets of ambiguities themselves, not readily apparent in English. The Greek terms employed could not only mean different things, but different words might or might not mean the same thing. This was so in everyday usage. When used of God, their meaning would be even harder to determine. The scope for confusion and misunderstanding between Greeks – let alone between Greeks and Latins – was enormous, and the Church took full advantage of it. The new language could scarcely begin to serve its intended purpose till the various ambiguities were ironed out. Yet its employment is profoundly significant. A precedent was set for the use of non-biblical language in the Christian confession of faith. This shows that what matters is not what language is used but how well it can serve to express the ultimacy of Jesus. Scriptural or non-scriptural language can be employed, whichever serves this purpose best.

For all the turmoil of the fourth century – with pagans complaining of the serious disruption of public transport due to so many priests hurrying to and from councils,[64] it might seem that at Nicaea, and more especially at Constantinople (AD 381), the patristic Church arrived at the point almost reached already in the New Testament, when not only were numerous symbols of transcendence and ultimacy applied to Jesus, but the risen Jesus, the Messiah, was all but identified with the Holy Spirit. Such language implied that the bearer of the name Jesus was none other than God in his continuing outreach. In the intervening years the Fathers had wrestled with the question – raised but not answered in the New Testament itself – of how Jesus could be one with God and yet distinct. Complete identification of Jesus with the Holy Spirit was ruled out by the New Testament record and the Church's memory of Jesus' historical life. It was this rather than the Logos' ancestry in Middle Platonism, which required the distinction to be maintained once the Logos was identified with Jesus.

In fact the identification of Jesus with the Spirit could not have proceeded further. As we saw, the witness of scripture told against it. Jesus himself simply was not Spirit without remainder; the mistake of docetism was to think that he was. Even as risen Lord he could only be 'all but' identified with the Spirit. In the gap created by the 'all but' he was not only distinguished from but still below God the Father. Another symbol was therefore needed which had the potential to bridge the gap in status without blurring the distinction. In other words, a way of expressing the ultimacy of Jesus was needed, that would proclaim him to be not just another inspired prophet but as having unique and exclusive transcendent status.

'Logos', for all its problems, ambiguities, and deficiencies, could serve that purpose. Combined with 'Son', it could lift Jesus to the orbit of Godhead, the point of unconditional ultimacy and universality.

The question now is whether, having served that purpose, this symbolic vehicle of exaltation, the Logos-Son, must remain locked to Jesus as the essential and eternal condition of his remaining in the heights, or whether it can now be seen as a vivid but limited metaphor which serves a crucial purpose but which can now be jettisoned and allowed to fall back to earth. It may be argued that it not only can but must be allowed to fall back, if the true and enduring meaning of Jesus' ultimacy is not to be obscured.

Right from the start the Logos-Son symbolism, for all its positive value, was never entirely free from negative implications. The Fathers, on their own assumptions concerning the inspiration of scripture, were committed to the identification of Jesus with the Logos as expressed in the Fourth Gospel. Given that fact, we can recognize that they struggled hard and at great cost to adjust their symbolic language to what they were convinced needed to be said about Jesus, rather than letting the symbols dictate and so distort the message. But it does not follow that they were entirely successful. Even after Nicaea and Constantinople, acute problems remained.

The Logos-Son symbol served the Church's need in pointing to Jesus' exalted status and hence his unique revelatory significance. But at the same time its incorporation into talk about Jesus introduced a complication into the originally straightforward portrayal in the Synoptic Gospels of Jesus' personal relationship with God his Father. In fact it would seem to have made such a relationship logically inconceivable. What could be said of the historical person, Jesus the Son, in relation to the Father could not at all easily be said of the pre-existent, divine Logos-Son and the Father. Besides the reality and limitations of his human experiences, the freedom of Jesus' response to God was the authentic expression of his humanity, without which he could have little to say to his fellow human beings.

The virtue of Arius' account was that at least his creaturely Logos had this freedom (hence his appeal, perhaps). But how could the freedom to turn from God, the corollary of the freedom to turn *to* God in love, be attributed to the co-eternal Logos-Son who was God himself by

Chapter 5

nature? To suggest such a thing would be to imply the possibility of self-contradiction in God, which is intolerable, or the possibility of sin in the Logos-Son, which was worse. At the same time, a genuine personal distinction within the eternal being of God would, as we have seen, either imply the existence of two Gods or require the subordination of one to the other.

The divine, eternally coexistent Logos had to be distinct from the Father because it was Jesus the Son, and yet could not be distinct in real personal terms without destroying the oneness of God and hence the principle of monotheism. The Church was reduced to affirming the distinction in terms of subtly defined metaphysical relationships, which excluded the possibility of real, mutual, personal relationship. Though it would continue to employ the language of personal relationship between Son and Father, particularly in the context of devotion, it had lost the logical basis for such language to be intelligible, or for such a relationship to be possible between the divine pre-existent Logos-Son and the Father. That being the case, it was not very difficult at this point to include the Holy Spirit as the third party to the relationship.

The real grounds for including the Spirit as a symbol of God's outreach were once again scriptural authority and the worshipping practice of the Church, especially, as noticed above, the Spirit's inclusion in the baptismal rite.[65] But the effect of doing so as an appendix to the debate about the Logos-Son was to incorporate the Spirit in very similar terms. The Logos had had to be differentiated from God and personalized because of its identification with Jesus and consequent designation as Son in relation to Father. There was no real need to individuate the Spirit in this sort of way, but the idea of distinction in unity postulated of the Logos-Son set a precedent for a similar distinction between the Spirit and God. Since the scriptural image of 'Son' was hardly appropriate in this case (the Spirit is never called Son!), some other differentiating term needed to be found, if possible one supported by the scriptures. So, while the Logos was described as *begotten*, the Spirit was described as *proceeding* (cf. John 15:26); and the distinction between begottenness and procession was left as the only differentiation between the Logos-Son and the Spirit, and also between these two and the Father in his unbegottenness.

All three were described as persons, that is, individuated realities. The word 'person' did not then have the connotation of personality or self-conscious identity, which in this context would seem to imply three Gods. The meaning of such distinctions was conceded to be an impenetrable

The Lordship of Christ and the language of Ultimacy

mystery.⁶⁶ In all other respects, the three persons were indissoluble and indistinguishable. The bare fact of their differentiation had to be accepted on the authority of scripture and Church councils.

The potentially destructive consequence of this intellectual impasse must be examined in due course, but first we must consider the relationship of the Logos as God to Jesus the man. This will bring us to the question of whether, here also, the interpolation of the Logos-Son symbol threatens the reality of Jesus' relationship with the Father, and whether we shall have to conclude that the reality of this relationship, and its centrality for faith, can only be recovered if the Logos-Son symbol is relinquished, or at least, if it is seen as a symbol expressing faith in Jesus' ultimacy, and no longer as designating a pre-existent divine being.

4. THE LOGOS AS GOD IN RELATION TO JESUS

The Church's refusal to let Jesus be less than God (less than ultimate) raised, as we have seen, the intractable question of the relationship of the Logos-Son to the Father. Its refusal to let go of Jesus' genuine humanity would raise an equally intractable question. How could the pre-existent, time-transcending Logos-Son who was God be identified with a man who was born and lived at a particular time and place?

Or how could the subject of a historical life be conceived to be a transcendent, spiritual, subjective reality. The identification of the Logos with Jesus raised this problem in an acute way. Different lines of thought developed in the Church, which once again may be associated with the traditions of Alexandria and Antioch.

(a) The Antiochenes

We have already mentioned the difficulty that the Antiochene theologians had in differentiating the Logos of God in Old Testament usage from God himself. To the extent that they could not distinguish the Logos from God, they could not identify it wholly with the historical Jesus. Their advantage then was that they could protect the Logos from 'unworthy' creaturely limitations and take seriously the reality of Jesus' humanity as portrayed in the New Testament, a life under the conditions and humiliations of historical existence and his free and authentic human response to God, in short, his freedom to love.

Had the more Jewish sense of 'Logos' as a symbol of God's purposive activity been preserved, the term might still have been available to them to express Jesus' revelatory uniqueness. By the time of Nicaea, however, the

Chapter 5

Antiochenes had allowed the symbol 'Son' to move from Jesus himself to the Logos,[67] so that the symbol of God's eternal purpose was transformed into a pre-existent, coeternal, personal being.[68] This Logos-Son was distinct from the Father by definition; yet, as sharing the Father's divine perfection, it was hard to see how he could be the subject of the very human experiences ascribed to Jesus in the New Testament, such as being tired, hungry, and ignorant, and facing real temptation. These experiences could not be predicated of God; but if they were unreal for Jesus – the Antiochenes were convinced – his true humanity would be denied, and consequently his redemptive work would count for nothing. The Logos-Son, distinct from the Father yet immune to human limitation, intervened awkwardly between Jesus and the Father, and could not be wholly identified with either. As their opponents were eager to point out, it was not easy for the Antiochenes to do full justice to the identification of Jesus with the Logos in the Fourth Gospel.

The question which arises from this is whether the Antiochenes, whatever their intentions, failed to establish the ultimate and universal significance of Jesus as the revelation of God. Could he be that, if he was not the Logos? Could he be anything more than an exceptionally inspired man at best? Or a kind of split personality with a dual subjectivity at worst, as the Alexandrians suspected?

The Antiochenes in fact tried very hard to meet objections, and to uphold Jesus' unique revelatory significance, by maintaining that the Logos was present and active in Jesus' life fully and continuously, whereas it was only present in other lives partially or temporarily.[69] Hence Jesus' uniqueness lay in the unique degree to which the Logos related to him and he to the Logos, and the degree was such that it amounted in effect to a qualitative distinction. It was in virtue of the presence and activity of the Logos in him from the very beginning of his life that Jesus could do God's work and be the true, final, and definitive revelation of God, without ceasing to be a truly human being.

If one were simply to substitute 'God' for 'Logos' here, or understand 'Logos' as a symbol for God in his outreach (which was more or less how the word was understood originally in the Antiochene tradition), the position summarized above would be very close to that put forward in this chapter. The argument here is that, as a consequence of his uniquely close and personal relationship with God, Jesus represented God faithfully, and in doing so confronted his own and later generations as the form of God.

However, the symbol 'Logos', tied to the pre-existent being, the Son, was no longer available to express the unique revelatory value of Jesus himself (in the way that 'Messiah' could originally). The Logos-Son had somehow to be a different subject from the subject of Jesus' historical human life. The Alexandrians, though their motives were less than generous and they could do little better themselves, nevertheless perceived the gap and with some justification concluded that in the Antiochene account there were either two subjects – two sons in Jesus, or else he was a mere man.[70]

The accusation contained an element of truth,[71] but was less than fair to Antiochene intentions and to another important aspect of their position. Unable to employ the Logos-symbol to identify Jesus as the revelation of God, the Antiochenes were left with the alternatives of denying this claim, which they did not wish to do, or of developing another term to serve this purpose. This they attempted to do with the Greek word *prosopon*. As argued above in the case of *homoousios*, it was a legitimate undertaking to resort to philosophical language to try to express the ultimate revelatory significance of Jesus, and not just to rely only on traditional symbols. The later Antiochenes, in particular Theodore of Mopsuestia and Nestorius, came very close to success with *prosopon*, and might perhaps have succeeded if their efforts had met with the serious theological attention they deserved instead of bitter personal vendettas and political manoeuvres, instigated primarily by Cyril of Alexandria.

The basic meaning of *prosopon* was 'face', and hence it had connotations of outward appearance, expression, and ultimately, of individual person as confronted. In other words, *prosopon* is virtually the equivalent of 'form' as we are using it. The import of Antiochene teaching was that to encounter the truly human historical, person, Jesus, was to encounter the *prosopon* of God himself – the invisible God visibly expressed in that human form. This, as an expression of faith in the revelatory significance of Jesus, clearly comes very close to our claim that in his genuine humanity Jesus was and is the form of God. One difference is that for the Antiochenes Jesus was the form of God throughout his lifetime and not only in the totality of his life, which could only be seen or grasped after his death. [72] However, the great value of their account is that it came very close to establishing that God can be represented in a human body and personal life – in other words, can be embodied or 'incarnated' – without the sacrifice of human authenticity.

Unfortunately, the Antiochenes lacked the courage of their convictions. They tended in practice to divide up the activity and words of Jesus as recorded in the New Testament between the personal Logos-Son and the man, implying after all a kind of split personality and divorcing God from what was truly human. The form of God was, it seems, to be seen not so much in the totality as in the parts. This practice seemed to confirm their opponents' worst fears. Perhaps the Antiochenes had little option, committed as they were to a pre-existent personified Logos, as well as to the reality of Jesus' human life.

The Antiochenes were also under another constraint, that of a pre-critical approach to Biblical exegesis. We can recognize now the problems this posed for them and for all their contemporaries. The difficulties of exegesis are still far from removed, but at least we can acknowledge now the human role in the creation of the New Testament. We can recognize that the combination and interweaving of historical record and theological interpretation in the pages of scripture does not necessarily represent the combination of a natural and a supernatural subject, as it were in harness in the one person of Jesus. This bears particularly on the interpretation of the Fourth Gospel, which was central to the debate.[73] Anyone compelled by their assumptions to take literally every word and experience attributed to Jesus in all the Gospels can hardly avoid either separating out what is human from what is divine in him, or else treating the human as more or less a pretence. That the Alexandrians leaned in the latter direction is not therefore something blameworthy, but neither are they to be considered exempt from criticism. Their grounds for criticizing the Antiochenes' failure to identify Jesus with the Logos may seem less valid now than in the past.

(b) The Alexandrians

In considering the Alexandrians' position, we find that their strength was the converse of the Antiochenes' weakness. There is, perhaps, even greater risk in generalizing about the former than the latter, but a number of shared convictions can be discerned in those who stood in the tradition of Athanasius. They agreed in condemning Arianism and in affirming that the Logos-Son was equal with God the Father and was born as Jesus. Hence Jesus had the full, unequivocal value of God, as the saving and revelatory figure of universal and ultimate significance. But he was that because the divine Logos-Son was deemed to be the subject of his life. Hence, in contrast to the Antiochenes, the Alexandrians (including Athanasius and Cyril) found it virtually impossible to take seriously, or at least to affirm intelligibly, the reality of Jesus' human existence.[74] At worst, a supernatural being simply took to himself a human body, not human existence, and his so-called human life was no more than a charade. His purpose would either be to use his flesh as disguise to fool and defeat the enemies of God, natural or supernatural, in order to save humankind (though it was very hard indeed to find convincing reasons why it should be done that way); or else through his divine power to divinize the flesh and/or the mind and so secure our salvation (but salvation in this account is at worst magical and subhuman, and at best divorced from the social and physical structures of earthly existence).

Two factors in this tradition stood in the way of complete denial of the reality of Jesus' human existence. One was the New Testament itself; the other was the slogan 'That which he has not assumed he has not healed'. The former witnessed to Jesus as a man, a particular person. The slogan, in contrast, served rather to affirm his humanity. The distinction is subtle but significant. The slogan, as formulated by Gregory of Nazianzus,[75] (one of a group of theologians known as the Cappadocian fathers), was effective in combating the extreme views of Apollinaris, Bishop of Laodicea[76] who frankly denied that Jesus had a human soul, or at least a human mind; its place was taken by the Logos. But Gregory's famous rejoinder affirmed it more as a matter of definition than as a dynamic, living reality. In this Christian Platonic tradition, the emphasis lay more on the Logos taking human nature or humanity to himself,[77] rather than becoming a man. A soul was a necessary constituent of human nature, and so part of the definition of humanity. Therefore the humanity which the Logos took must have included a soul. But where 'soul' is merely part of a definition, its role is passive. This leaves the Logos free to be the active subject of Jesus' life.

This neat solution could not, however, satisfy Apollinaris or the Antiochenes. Despite their opposition to each other, they both agreed that a passive soul is no real soul at all. In this account, the Logos did the work; the human soul, like the Holy Spirit, could have nothing in particular to do apart from just being there. Least of all could this passive soul be conceived of as a genuine subject capable of a free and mutual personal relationship with the Logos-Son or God the Father. To imagine that, or to ascribe any special functions to 'it', apart from those ascribed to the Logos in Jesus, would at once conjure up an image of a split personality in him, or at least a strange sort of double life. This is exactly what the Alexandrians objected to in the Antiochene view; yet in the end even Cyril began to admit a specific role for Jesus' human soul.[78] The difficulty of avoiding such an implication, where there was still concern to affirm Jesus' humanity, is a symptom of the tension generated by the conflict

Chapter 5

between the logic of the Logos-Son symbol and the New Testament picture of Jesus as a real man.

In the last resort, the idea of a duality of subjective identities in Jesus (the Logos-Son and the man) was as intolerable as a duality of subjective identities in God (the Father and the Logos-Son) Yet without this, though Jesus' humanity might be affirmed in theory, no real or active role could be conceded to it for fear of displacing his 'Godness' as Logos or of splitting his personality. In a sincere attempt to overcome the problem, the idea of exchange of attributes (*communicatio idiomatum*)[79] was introduced, but in practice, in the later history of the Church, the reality of Jesus' human existence has constantly tended to give way to the idea that the subject of his historical life was a supernatural pre-existent being, the Logos-Son, distinct from God the Father but sharing with him such attributes of divinity as omnipotence and omniscience, far removed from the limitations of human life as we experience it. His mother could seem more real and approachable as a fellow human being.

(c) Chalcedon

The Church had struggled for centuries to express its faith in the ultimacy of Jesus, sometimes presenting him as God, but not quite human, or human, but not quite God. The debate came to a head in AD 451 at the Council of Chalcedon (across the Bosporus, opposite Constantinople). The reality of Jesus' humanity and of his divinity was affirmed in the definition issued at the Council, but without explanation as to how humanity and divinity were integrated in the life and person of Jesus. Further disputes arose subsequently as to whether one or two wills were present and operative in Jesus. This only serves to underline the inherent problem posed by attributing to Jesus a transcendent subjectivity distinct from a genuine human subjectivity.

We have already seen how the Logos identified with Jesus was held to be distinct from God, and yet incapable of a fully personal relationship with God of the kind which the Synoptic Gospels particularly depict between Jesus and the Father. Still less could there be a reciprocal, personal relationship between the human nature and the divine nature in the person of the historical Jesus as defined after Chalcedon.

Thus we see how, in the course of the Church's debate about Jesus, the question of the relationship between Jesus and his heavenly Father became two questions concerning the relationship between the Logos-Son and God the Father, and the Logos-Son and Jesus. Neither relationship could

The Lordship of Christ and the language of Ultimacy

be truly free and personal. The Logos-Son identified with Jesus and equal with God could indeed serve to affirm Jesus' ultimacy and so to uphold Jesus' revelatory significance, and through him God's free, personal, and loving outreach to all humankind and the whole of creation. But this primary objective of faith could, it seems, only be purchased at the price of Jesus' genuine, evolutionary, historical reality, and his freedom to respond as an authentic human being to God. Without that, the case for Jesus' revelatory significance today falls to pieces – he would not be one of us.

The symbol 'Logos', better than 'Spirit' or 'Wisdom', could serve a purpose in the Greek world analogous to the idea of 'Messiah' in the Jewish world in affirming and proclaiming Jesus as the definitive revelation of God. 'Logos' with its different connotations, in conjunction with 'Son' and enriched by 'Wisdom', created a picture of Jesus as God's agent and representative in the sphere of creation, yet not as a subordinate being but equal with God himself. It may be suggested that the underlying conviction represented here is identical with that expressed in the phrases 'Jesus is the form of God' or 'God is in the form of Jesus'. However, the personification of the Logos symbol generated acute problems, both conceptual and practical.

Further problems may be seen to arise from the fact that, though 'Logos' could take the place of 'Messiah', their connotations were by no means identical. 'Logos' could symbolize not only Jesus as the form of God, but Jesus in his spiritual role as the life-giving source of divine power in human experience. The use of 'Logos' with this wider meaning instead of 'Messiah' meant that the equilibrium of 'Messiah' and 'Spirit' as symbols of the form and vitality of God in Jesus was upset. The combination of both poles in 'Logos' left 'Spirit' in an equivocal position. At the same time, though the designation 'only begotten Son' had marked Jesus out as unique, the transference of Son to Logos weakened the uniqueness of Jesus inasmuch as the Logos-Son could 'speak' in others. Another consequence of identifying Jesus as Logos rather than Messiah was equally serious, if not more so.

The term 'Messiah' had a meaning, but had not hitherto had personal application, and so could be applied to Jesus, but that this was not entirely without difficulty may be gathered from the episode recorded in Matthew 16: 13–23 as noted above (p. 77). Peter's acknowledgement of Jesus as Messiah, as God's special agent, was accepted by Jesus, it seems; but Peter's subsequent insistence that Jesus as Messiah must not suffer and die was sharply rebuked – 'Get thee behind me, Satan! ... You think as men think, not as God thinks.' (NEB) We have here a good example of a symbol of transcendence serving two purposes. On the one hand it could be used to good effect to express faith in the ultimacy of Jesus. On the other hand, its content had to be corrected in the light of what Jesus was and did, instead of Jesus being made to fit into current preconceptions associated with Messiahship.[80]

In comparison, Logos could be assimilated with the risen Lord – Jesus in the Spirit – relatively easily, but the assimilation of Logos, conceived of as a pre-existent being, with the historical Jesus was almost impossible. The resulting paradox was that the risen Jesus-Logos could scarcely be identified with the Jesus who lived a human life and died. 'Logos' served a positive purpose in a way analogous to 'Messiah' in signifying the closeness of Jesus' relationship to God and his role as the expression of God's creative purpose. But latter-day Peters would take Jesus-Logos aside and rebuke him, saying he could not even be a human being, let alone suffer and die, and Jesus was not there to rebuke them.

The New Testament was there, however, as an obstinate witness to Jesus' genuine human life and death. It still is. Those who imagine that the role of expressing God's creative purpose could not be fulfilled in a truly human life are still rebuked for thinking as men think, and not allowing their thoughts to be reshaped radically enough by what Jesus was and did. They fail to take the Incarnation seriously enough, even when their intention is to uphold the conviction that God was in Jesus.

To conclude. The temptation to conform Jesus to presuppositions concerning Logos was very strong. The symbol 'Son', through its assimilation to 'Wisdom', had all but slipped its historical moorings, and so could do little to keep Logos subject to historical reality. As a result, the continuity between the human Jesus and the risen Lord represented by the resurrection stories was all but broken. The identification of Jesus' selfhood with the selfhood of a pre-existent spiritual being (Logos-Son) tended to divorce Jesus worshipped as Logos-Son from the concrete figure of flesh and blood portrayed in the Gospels.

Jesus' experience of human life, his freedom as a responsible human being to wrestle with and take difficult decisions, even his suffering and death, have been rendered so unreal by generations of Christian piety that the impact of his originality, integrity, courage, and inspiring dedication to God has all too often been virtually lost to sight. Alternatively, where these things were counted real, it was as though the suffering he was ready to bear was real for the man but not for God, as though it was not precisely there, in the form of Jesus who was and is the form of God, that the quality of God's love was disclosed. If these criticisms have any validity, then we cannot rest content with the attempts of the early Fathers to express the ultimacy of Jesus. The utter seriousness of their commitment is witnessed to by their constant willingness to undergo suffering, exile, or martyrdom, rather than deny their convictions.[81] But this does not of itself guarantee the adequacy of their words and language to convey what needed to be conveyed.

Commitment to the ultimacy of Jesus today therefore requires Christians to try as hard as their forbears in the early Church to confess their commitment to him and to communicate what they believe to be true about him as best they can in our world and in terms of our way of thinking. They must also recognize that they have less excuse than their Christian forebears for refusing to re-examine or to let go of symbols or images that are not adequate to their purpose, if that purpose is understood to mean witnessing to the ultimacy of the man Jesus. If need be, even the most hallowed symbols, such as 'Logos-Son', must be relinquished, or at least submitted to stringent re-examination. But whatever symbols may be resorted to in order to express Jesus' ultimacy, however positive their value, Jesus' followers must, like Peter, allow themselves to be rebuked by what Jesus was, if they are to serve his purposes.

5. CHALCEDON REAPPRAISED

It would be impossible in the space available here to pursue our historical inquiry further, but neither is it really necessary, for two reasons. In the first place, we have argued that the fundamental compulsion of the first disciples and their successors in the early Church was to proclaim the ultimacy of Jesus. If that view is valid, then we may hope that our examination of their attempts to articulate and communicate their convictions will at least have served to identify some of the principles and problems which will attend any attempt to express Jesus' ultimacy, and which are not only relevant to the early period of the Church's history. In the second place, though the Church's struggle to articulate its convictions did not end when the patristic period drew to a close (and never can end), nevertheless the Council of Chalcedon was a major watershed. The definition of faith promulgated there drew together in terms of the prevailing symbol-system the essential elements of commitment to Jesus. It affirmed his historical reality (humanity) and his ultimacy (divinity), but denied division in God or in Jesus himself.

Chapter 5

As we have seen, the terms in which these convictions were expressed generated acute intellectual problems, but nevertheless they were to serve as the main basis for the articulation of Christian commitment in the future, especially in the West. This fact means that a reassessment of the position reached at Chalcedon, and the way it was arrived at, creates a new point of departure for theological reflection.

The next task therefore, and one beyond the scope of this chapter, would be to draw out implications, both theological and practical, of the position argued here. In the concluding section I will attempt to answer the immediate question, 'What should those who respond to Jesus today say about him, about God, and about the Holy Spirit?'

It is my contention that the early Church upheld the fundamental commitment to Jesus which it inherited from his first followers, but that it failed to resolve the contradictions into which it was drawn by the symbols it employed within the prevailing conceptual framework. But even its failure witnesses to its primary commitment. It preferred the embarrassment of unresolved contradictions to the respectability of a coherent but one-sided representation of its convictions. One might perhaps say that at Chalcedon the Church preserved the vital parts, but the best it could do was to put them in a tidy pile, like the pieces of a jigsaw puzzle sorted out and neatly stacked, but not put together.

Such reservations about the achievement of Chalcedon will not be shared by all. The mystery with which we are concerned is such that it would certainly be extremely presumptuous to suppose that the puzzle can be completed here. But it may still be legitimate to look at the pieces again to see if some at least could be rearranged and fitted together in a way that will allow something more of the picture to emerge – a picture of which we ourselves and our evolutionary world are an integral part. With that assumption I shall now attempt to offer a brief outline of how the pieces might be handled on the basis of the approach which has governed this inquiry.

In the previous sections it was argued that the 'Logos-Son' symbol played an invaluable role in pointing to the ultimate significance of Jesus; but at the same time we saw how the identification of Jesus with the Logos-Son, as if with a pre-existent spiritual being, generated a great many of the difficulties which confronted the Church in its earliest days and has done ever since. The problem of relating the Logos-Son to the Father, to the Holy Spirit, and to the human Jesus was and remains intractable.

The term 'Logos' itself admittedly fell largely out of use for a number of reasons, and was replaced by almost exclusive use of the symbol 'Son'. It is sometimes argued that the problems associated with the Logos-concept were removed when the term was relinquished. To some extent this may be conceded, inasmuch as the connotations of 'Son' can be derived more directly from the New Testament portrayal of Jesus, and are less tied to outside usage than was the case with 'Logos'. Nevertheless, we may say that by the time 'Son' displaced 'Logos' the damage had been done. 'Son' had by then acquired the connotations of a pre-existent spiritual subject. It was this spiritual being, the second person of the Trinity, descending 'from above', which was conceived of as taking flesh and so becoming incarnate in Jesus. So far from this being the truth by which membership of the Church should be defined, I would hold that this account not only creates an intellectual impasse, but obstructs the response of others to the ultimacy of Jesus and obscures its implications.

The way through this impasse may lie in abandoning the identification of Jesus with the Logos, or with Wisdom, or with Son, *as if* with a pre-existent spiritual being, distinct from God. The symbols 'Logos', 'Wisdom', and 'Son' can then all be subordinated to the person of Jesus – as was the case with 'Messiah' – instead of their subordinating him to their connotations and logic. Logos may then be interpreted not as a personal being in itself, but as 'the principle of divine self-manifestation'[82] or, as I suggest, 'the form of God'. The word can then function in a positive sense, analogous to that of 'Messiah', pointing to the unique, universal and ultimate revelatory significance of Jesus, without implying a duality of selfhood in him any more than would be implied by calling him 'Messiah'. Thus, as Messiah, Jesus is the one who performs God's work of salvation. As Logos (or Wisdom), he is the one who brings God to light (John 1:9) and renders the eternal truth of God visible, apprehensible, and communicable.

This interpretation allows us to recover the original significance and force of the symbol 'Son', which pointed to that relationship between Jesus and God which made it possible for him to reveal God and so to be for us the form of God. At last we can escape the problems posed by the merely quasi-filial relationship between God and the Logos, which could not be differentiated in a fully personal way without the risk of polytheism. We can abandon also the almost mechanical, impersonal relationship between the divine nature (Logos) and the human nature (flesh and perhaps soul) of Jesus, which could not be thought of as a personal relationship for fear of splitting Jesus in half.

Chapter 5

The impersonality of the latter view led only too easily to an impersonal view of the relationship between God and human beings. It lent itself to the idea of divine substance divinizing human substance,[83] in contrast to a personal understanding of the creative interactions of love between God and human persons. It was to these creative interactions that the New Testament bore witness; they have persisted among Jesus' followers despite doctrinal formulations rather than because of them. The recovery of the idea of sonship in the fully personal relationship of Jesus to the Father may disclose possibilities for Jesus' fellow human beings which have been rendered all too remote by metaphysical abstractions and mythological intrusions. At the same time, the designation of Jesus as the form of God would uphold his unique relationship to God and his distinction from all other human beings, without sacrificing his humanity.

Thus, by interpreting Logos in this way and not as a pre-existent being, we are free from the logical constraints which made it so hard for the Alexandrians to acknowledge a real human being to be the form of God. We are free to recover Jesus as a man whose life was woven into the fabric of creation, evolution, human history, and society, as much as any other human being's. Paradoxically, the recognition of this man as the form of God may be reckoned to impart a profounder significance to the ancient symbol of incarnation than does the traditional view. The very word, 'enfleshment', gives itself away, isolating the physical from the social and historical, contrary to what we now recognize as constituting a human person. Despite professions to the contrary, the traditional view cannot represent Jesus coherently as of ultimate revelatory significance and yet at the same time fully implicated in all the many strands of human existence.[84]

The next question is whether the interpretation presented here, whatever its worth, parts company with the conclusions reached at Chalcedon to such a degree that no real connection or continuity can be claimed. Or does this re-sorting of. the pieces in fact allow something more of the original picture to emerge? I would wish to defend the latter alternative. In order to do so, we must develop further a distinction which has already been implicit in what has been said, but which needs to be made explicit – the distinction between confessional and descriptive language, and the way each functions.

The traditional designations of Jesus – 'Messiah', 'Lord', 'Logos', 'Wisdom', and 'Son of God' as interpreted here, all emerge not as descriptive but as confessional symbols, that is, as expressions of faith in the ultimate revelatory significance of Jesus as the form of God. He was believed to have been in a right relationship with God and thus to have become for all human beings the norm of a right relationship with God, superseding all other supposed norms. It is the logic of this confession that must be explored.

If it is the truth of God that has appeared in Jesus, then it is a truth relevant to all things in every time and place, and no less valid for not being recognized as such in every time and place.[85] This claim does not imply that the truth of God in Jesus can be fully and perfectly expressed in verbal form. It is a judgement of faith that the truth of God was in Jesus, but this judgement is not and was not arrived at arbitrarily in a historical vacuum. Where it is made, it means that in principle Jesus is deemed to be (and so confessed to be) the criterion of truth, and that in practice the story of Jesus serves as the normative interpretative resource for the understanding of God, however tentative and contingent the conclusions drawn from the available evidence.

On the basis of these observations we may now reconsider some of the central problems of Christology, starting with the supposed sinlessness and eternal changelessness of Jesus. No historical evidence can ever serve to prove (or disprove) that Jesus was sinless. We can, however, make sense of this traditional belief about Jesus on the basis of the distinction between descriptive and confessional language.

Faith confesses Jesus to be the criterion of truth. He cannot be my criterion and not my criterion of truth simultaneously (even though I could be wrong). From the perspective of faith, then, it would be self-contradictory to confess that Jesus was and is the truth, the norm of right relationship with God, and *at the same time* to concede that he was wrong about God, or in a fundamentally wrong relationship, that is, a sinner. Hence, in confessional language, Jesus must be sinless; in this language his sinlessness is logically necessary corollary of ultimacy. It is a way of saying that he is the criterion of truth.[86]

The eternal changelessness of Jesus can similarly be seen to have a place in the language of confession. It would be incompatible with the conviction that Jesus was the truth of God to suppose that the truth which Jesus bodied out only became true during his ministry, as if the truth of God only came into being then. This would be absurd. What we can say is that the truth of God is conterminous with God, but was bodied out in time in the person of Jesus, not as a third person, but as eternal truth made visible.

Thus, the terms 'sinless', 'changeless', 'eternal', belong to Jesus confessed as the form of God, as the *locus* of revelation. But such terms cannot, without confusion, be transposed from the confession of Jesus as the form of God to descriptions of Jesus as the person he was. Some description is necessary, or else the confession would be devoid of content, but what can be said of a genuine human being, and of Jesus in particular, is not to be confused with the language and logic of commitment to Jesus as the form of God.

This claim, that Jesus is the form of God, can of course be challenged by anyone at any time, and even those who respond to him as such may well entertain doubts. But our concern thus far is with the logic or function of confessional language, not with the psychology of the confessor, or even at this point with the problems of the historian. When, however, we turn to consider Jesus as the man he was, our fellow human being, we can readily acknowledge in him the same conditions of human existence as are found in all of us, the experience of changing, growing, learning, loving, meeting temptation, and exercising human responsibility.

To describe Jesus as sinless in this context is simply to report the conviction of his followers not that he was never angry with his brothers and sisters or even his mother, but that he remained faithful to his vocation in the face of real trials and temptation (Heb. 4:15) and that his vocation was indeed God's calling. This triumphant sinlessness of Jesus is the foundation of the confession; it is not nullified by the necessary sinlessness which belongs to confession. Very serious problems arise when the logical necessities of confessional language are transposed into descriptive language. Tension between confession and psychological description was the problem for the early Church. Tension between confession and historical description has been added to this in the last century and a half.

When ideas which have their roots in unconditional commitment are treated on the plane of empirical observation, they result in a demand for certainty in historical terms which historical judgement cannot reach beyond probabilities at best. Thus, the confusion of languages undermines the integrity of historical inquiry. The product of the confusion of languages in the case of Jesus is the contradiction of a non-historical being living historically. One-sided resolutions result in an account of Jesus as just one man among others, or in a portrayal of him as incapable of growing in wisdom and understanding (Luke 2:52), immune to temptation and unable to sin. If that were so, he was not free and was therefore subhuman – not one of us.

Having, then, the distinction between confession and description in mind, we may recognize that the early Fathers were necessarily concerned with both, but with different emphases, depending in part on their different understanding of human nature, of what Jesus had done, and how he had effected salvation. In very general terms it might be said that the Alexandrians tended to subordinate everything to the logic of confession. Given their Platonic presuppositions, the tensions of which we have spoken would not have seemed as acute to them as to us. Salvation was won by the divine Logos-Son taking humanity to himself, not by a moral victory.

The Antiochenes, on the other hand, with their different presuppositions, were more concerned to preserve the content of the New Testament description of Jesus as a human being and moral agent, as well as to confess him as the truth of God. Salvation was won by Jesus' genuine obedience to the Father. When at Alexandria the necessary sinlessness of Jesus as the form of God (Logos) was applied to Jesus as a man, he ceased to be truly human (as far as their account went, if not their intentions). But at Antioch, as we have seen, the real human Jesus could not quite be presented as the form of God (even if that was intended).

Thus, as we have argued, Chalcedon in affirming both traditions preserved the essentials of confessional language and the description of Jesus as a historical human being, but failed to resolve the apparent contradictions. By removing from the symbol 'Logos' the connotation of a pre-existent personal being, and by interpreting it as synonymous with the form of God, we can see the possibility of resolving the contradictions of Chalcedon and reconciling the concerns of Alexandria and Antioch.

We may reinterpret the Alexandrians' identification of the second person of the Trinity with the subject of Jesus' life, seeing it rather as an expression of faith in the ultimacy of Jesus in the most unequivocal terms open to them. The phrase 'Jesus is Logos-Son' can then be seen to be confessional rather than descriptive, echoing the New Testament confessions 'Jesus is Lord' and 'Jesus is Messiah', but introducing even higher connotations of ultimacy. Jesus, the man who lived a real human life in history would be that, as against something else momentarily appearing in a historical figure.

Arius' emphasis on the reality of Jesus' moral freedom and the Antiochenes' insistence on his genuine humanity would be vindicated, and would be no more incompatible with the confession of his ultimacy than recognizing Jesus as the carpenter from Galilee was incompatible with acknowledging him to be Messiah and Lord. But the supposed failure to distinguish Jesus unequivocally in terms of his unique revelatory significance from all other human beings would be overcome.

Chapter 5

It is not being suggested here that the interpretation given above is all that the early Fathers really intended and meant. That would certainly be untrue, and very different interpretations of them can be given today. However, whatever their intentions, my case is that the distinctions we have drawn can be discerned in the formularies of the early Church, and that the question of the *ultimacy* of the *man* Jesus can be seen as the fundamental issue over which the Church was wrestling, both in its internal controversies and in relation to other religions and worldly powers. If these convictions are the pieces, then it can at least be argued that the picture we are trying to construct is essentially the same as that which preoccupied the early Fathers, even if it is being assembled in a somewhat different way.

Those who in the early Church responded in faith to Jesus as ultimate struggled for centuries to express that faith not only in the face of martyrdom and persecution but in the face of the seemingly insurmountable logical and philosophical obstacles imposed on them by the conceptual framework in which their lives were set. The greatest obstacle of all, I suggest, was the prevailing Biblical and philosophical assumption that there was one God. This as we have seen, appeared to require that Father and Son were one thing, or that the Son was subordinate to Father. To their credit, the early Fathers after centuries of bitter struggle, finally realized that it was God himself who had to be deconstructed, or more correctly, that the concept of God would have to be redefined, if the ultimacy of Jesus was to be upheld in relation to God, the ground and goal of all things.

The confession 'Thou art the Messiah' could extend to 'Thou art the Logos-Son' and reach its limit with the ultimately unsurpassable symbol of transcendence, 'Thou art God'. But warned by Jesus' rebuke to Peter, we must take care not to continue with 'that means you can't be fully human' or 'if you are fully human, you can't really be God in the strict sense, only as a courtesy title', or, back to Peter, 'if you are truly God, you can't possibly suffer and die.'

Peter had to learn that if Jesus was the Messiah, Messiahship did not exclude suffering and death. Jesus' followers had to learn that if Jesus was God, Godship was not a singularity that excluded differentiation. From this discovery emerged the doctrine of the Trinity, which one might describe as the ontological precondition of the Lordship of Jesus and his saving work in time. 'God' as perceived in the Old Testament or in philosophy simply could not fit or measure up to what Christians felt they had to say about the ultimacy of Jesus.

The Lordship of Christ and the language of Ultimacy

Behind all the debates and controversies, we may find that the profoundest confession of faith in the ultimacy of Jesus is simply 'Jesus is Lord!' The ontological corollary of that confession – what must be true about God, about Jesus, about ourselves and our world, if that confession is true and rightly made, is a matter of legitimate inquiry. As we have already noted, the intellectual implications of this confession are the subject matter of academic theology; the practical implications are the subject matter of Christian ethics. Though distinct, these two branches are inseparable (as can be seen already in the letters of Paul). The immediate source of Christian understanding and life is the written witness to Jesus' impact on the lives of his followers provided in the New Testament and by Jesus' followers down the ages. Their ultimate source is the mysteriously elusive and yet ultimate object of Christian faith, Jesus of Nazareth.

I have explored the ways in which the early Christians struggled to express the ultimacy of Jesus. In doing so they inevitably raise the question of Jesus' standing in relation to other faiths. That issue always lay in the background even if it was not always at the forefront of theological interest. However, today it is at the forefront and a matter of vital importance. It is to this issue that I now turn.

Notes
1 This chapter is a revised version of part IV in my book *Form and Vitality in the World and God* (Oxford, 1985). Its central thesis was that God is revealed objectively in the form of Jesus, and subjectively (or experientially) in the vitality of the Spirit. Both dimensions (or polarities) must be encompassed in an adequate account of revelation.

2 Dunn 1980, 144, *'for Paul as much as for the earlier Jewish writers the Spirit is the dynamic power of God himself reaching out to and having its effect on men'* (emphasis original).

3 'The thought of the earliest Fathers about God was at least as much binitarian as trinitarian' (Wiles 1976, 9). See also Wiles 1967, 79 f.

4 Some early writers even identified Jesus with the Holy Spirit. See Lampe 1977, 114; Grillmeier 1975, 56 (quoting the 2nd century Apostolic Father, Hermas), 'The Holy Spirit, which was there beforehand, which created all creation, was made by God to dwell in the fleshly nature which he willed' (*Similitudes*, v. 6. 5). Cf. Also Cyprian's description of the Incarnation, 'The Holy Spirit puts on flesh, God is mingled with man' (*Idol*. 11), quoted by Lampe 1976, 211.

5 See Williams 1985, 184. See Baruch 4:1, Ecclesiasticus 24:1–23, cf. John 1:1–14.

6 Dunn 1980, 196, '*...the first Christians were ransacking the vocabulary available*

Chapter 5

to them in order that they might express as fully as possible the significance of Jesus' (emphasis original).

7 See Lampe 1977, 35.

8 See Harvey 1982, 78.

9 Shürer 1979, 505; also Dunn 1980, 72, 75–82. (Jer. 1:4 shows how the sense of a divinely foreordained destiny can be expressed in language that might suggest pre-existence). Dunn holds that there is no idea of a pre-existent Christ in Paul's thought, even in Phil. 2:6–11 (Dunn 1980, 114–21). For a contrary view, see Hengel 1976, 66 ff.

10 Or exceptionally two, as at Qumran, where the kingly Messiah of David and the priestly Messiah of Aaron had complementary roles. However this left an unresolved tension over the question of ultimacy. See Vermes 1977, 184 ff.

11 Grant 1971, 106. Cf. Wilken 1984, 118–21.

12 Dunn 1980, 182 and *passim*.

13 Lampe (1977) might seem to run this risk (e.g. p. 145). And as a result be exposed to a charge of unitarianism, but in terms of the present argument his repeated emphasis on the normativeness of Jesus defends him from this charge (pp. 34, 64, 106, 114, 181).

14 Grillmeier 1975, 88 n. 183.

15 2 John 7. See Brown 1979, 113 f. for the party attacked in the Johannine epistles.

16 Grillmeier 1975, 76 f.

17 Kähler 1964, 66, '*The real Christ is the Christ who is preached*' (emphasis original); quoted in Kummel 1973, 224. See also Harvey 1967, 173–9.

18 See above, n. 5.

19 Lampe 1977, 132.

20 Dunn 1980, 163–212.

21 Ibid., 176.

22 Dunn 1980 rejects even this possibility: p. 210, '*Wisdom never really became more than a convenient way of speaking about God acting in creation, revelation and salvation*' (emphasis original).

23 Ibid., 194

24 'Gnostic' (derived from the Greek gnosis) is the name given to the varied dualistic and syncretistic religious movements which flourished in the second century AD. Apart from distancing God from creation, they ascribe an intermediate status to Christ and consequently denied his ultimacy. See Rudolph 1983.

25 Rare individuals who were acknowledged to be in exceptionally close relationship to God. See Vermes 1973.

26 If ideas of pre-existent sonship already existed (cf. Hengel 1976), at the very least these would have been strongly reinforced by the combination of symbols in Jesus.

27 Liddell and Scott 1883. Logos can mean verbal expression, particular utterance, or divine oracle; it is rarely used for a single word (ibid., 9th edn., 1940).

28 See Dunn 1980, 217–20.

29 These movements stemmed from the revival of Platonism in the 1st century BC, and flourished in the 2nd century AD until the emergence of Neoplatonism with Plotinus. For a full account, see Dillon 1977. For a brief introduction, see Norris 1966, 8–32; also Armstrong 1957, 147–55.

30 For an exhaustive treatment of Plato, see Guthrie 1975 and 1978. For a concise introduction, see Hare 1982.

31 See Guthrie 1981; also Barnes 1982.

32 Hare 1982, 30, 'One of Plato's chief incentives to metaphysics was a nest of problems which he thought he had encountered about knowledge.'

33 Guthrie 1975, iv. 507, 'Absolute standards of right and wrong could only be restored along with belief in a world of stable and comprehensible reality…supreme reality is supreme goodness.' Also Hare 1982, 18.

34 Guthrie 1978, 378, 'By the theory of Forms I mean the idea that what we call universals are not simply concepts in the mind, but objective realities displaying their character to perfection and eternally, invisible to the senses, but grasped after intensive preparation by a sort of intellectual vision, with an existence independent of their unstable and imperfect instances or copies which are all that we experience in this life.' Also Hare 1982, 32–7.

35 Timaeus, 3–4 (trans. Lee, Harmondsworth, 1965). Also Norris 1966, 16–22; Guthrie 1978, 253 ff.

36 See Norris 1966, 22 f.; also Armstrong 1957, 119–29.

37 e.g. Antiochus of Ascalon, a philosopher of the first century BC (Dillon 1977, 83). Philo and Plutarch (1st and early 2nd centuries AD) frequently refer to the Logos in this sense (Dillon 1977, 159, 200).

38 e.g. Atticus and Albinus (2nd century AD) (Dillon 1977, 252, 284).

39 Ibid. 115.

40 Ibid. 127 f.

41 Hare 1982, 10 f.

42 Guthrie 1981, 252–62 (p. 259, 'The first Unmoved Mover is God'). Also Dillon 1977, 13; Armstrong 1957, 88–91.

43 Guthrie 1975. 503–21.

44 Dillon 1977, 48, 'With the assimilation of the Platonic Demiurge (World Soul) to the Stoic Logos, the situating of the Ideas in the mind of God becomes more or less inevitable.' This probably occurred with Antiochus of Ascalon or even earlier.

45 In its philosophical context, the Logos is a metaphysical principle rather than a personal being, though metaphorical language could blur the distinction.

46 Kelly 1977, 95–9, 111 f.

47 For Philo as a Middle Platonist, see Dillon 1977, 139–83. For the place of Logos in Gnostic speculations, see Rudolph 1983. He attaches more importance to Gnostic influences on early Christian theology than I do.

48 For the contrasting approaches to biblical exegesis, see Wiles on Origen

Chapter 5

and Theodore of Mopsuestia, in Ackroyd and Evans (eds.) 1970, 454–510 (p. 489, '[Antiochene] emphasis on the biblical text, on historical fact and on the humanity of Jesus'). See also Wallace-Hadrill 1982, 31 f.

49 Grillmeier 1975, 88 n. 183, with reference to Justin, Hippolytus, and Tertullian.

50 Detailed treatment of the development of Logos-theology can be found in Grillmeier 1975 and Kelly 1977.

51 See Wiles 1967.

52 The shift of meaning from adoption to natural sonship in the case of Jesus may have already begun with Paul, perhaps under the pressure of Wisdom imagery; cf. Gal. 4:4.

53 '...like a battle by night', according to the historian Socrates (c. 380–c. 450 AD). *Hist. Eccl.* i. 23.

54 Athanasius *De Synodis*, 15. See Gregg and Groh 1981, 96 and *passim*.

55 Gregg and Groh 1981, 102 f.; cf. Kelly 1977, 229.

56 Ibid., 84.

57 This is Gregg and Groh's main thesis.

58 Chadwick 1967, 130.

59 Lietzman 1950, 117.

60 See Kelly 1977, 233–7.

61 The views of later Arians differed in important respects from those of Arius, but they shared his concern to preserve the transcendent oneness of God. For a detailed account, see Kelly 1977, 237–69; Chadwick 1967, 133–51; and Young 1983, 109–15 and *passim*. The last enlarges very usefully on the background and personalities of the protagonists.

62 Gregg and Groh 1981, 30, 49, 52, and esp. 56, 'One equal to the Son, the Superior is able to beget' (from Arius' *Thalia*).

63 See Wiles 1967, 96.

64 The emperor Constantine II was held responsible, 'He ruined the establishment of public conveyances by devoting them to the service of crowds of priests, who went to and fro to different synods, as they call the meetings at which they endeavour to settle everything according to their own fancy' (Ammianus Marcellinus, *Res Gestae*, xxi.16.18, quoted in Stevenson (ed.) 1966, 3.

65 Wiles 1967, 80 f.

66 'The begetting of God must be honoured by silence. It is a great thing for you to learn that he was begotten. But the manner of his generation we will not admit that even angels can conceive, much less you' (Gregory of Nazianzus, *3rd Theol. Oration*, 8; in Hardy (ed.) 1954, 65).

67 Pollard 1970, I.19, on Eustathius of Antioch.

68 Gregg and Groh 1981, 2, 'Dr. Robert Sample has shown... that one of the major results of the Synod of Antioch of AD 268 was to render automatically suspect any theological system without a pre-existent cosmological Christ.'

69 Grillmeier 1975, 429–39 (on Theodore of Mopsuestia); 457–63 (on Nestorius); also Young 1983, 199–213, 229–40.

70 Cyril, *Letter to Acacius*, 15, 'Nestorius...makes a pretence of affirming that the Word was incarnate and became man whilst being God, and failing to recognise the meaning of being incarnate he uses the words 'two natures' but sunders them from each other, isolating God and a separate man connected with God in a relation only of equal honour and sovereignty' (Wickham 1983, 51; cf. p. 65, 'To Eulogius').

71 Grillmeier 1975, 431, 459–63.

72 See Williams 1985, 211 f.

73 See Barrett 1978.

74 Young 1983, 261, 'Basically, however, Cyril regarded the whole matter as beyond human explanation and yet still true; paradox is the best way of stating such truths.' See pp. 213–29, 240–65, for a fuller account of Cyril; also Grillmeier 1975, 414–17, 473–83.

75 Gregory of Nazianzus, 'Letter to Cledonius against Apollinaris' (Epistle 101), in Hardy 1954. See Kelly 1977, 297.

76 See Kelly 1977, 289–95; Young 1983, 182–91.

77 Hare 1982, 46, 'Whereas for us a definition is one kind of analytically or necessarily true proposition, for [Plato] it was a description of a mentally visible and eternally true object.'

78 '2nd letter to Succensus' (Wickham 1983, 84–93). Cf. Grillmeier 1975, 474 ff.

79 For Gregory of Nazianzuz use of the concept, see Kelly 1977, 294.

80 Cf. Pannenberg's distinction between Christology 'from below' and 'from above': 1968, 33–7.

81 In the words of one of the most famous 'heretics', Nestorius, who suffered worse than most, 'Now my death approaches and every day I pray to God to dismiss me – me whose eyes have seen the salvation of God. Rejoice with me, Desert, thou my friend, my nurse, my home; and thou exile, my mother, who after my death will keep my body until the resurrection by the grace of God' (quoted in Young 1983, 240).

82 Tillich 1978, ii. 95.

83 Ibid., 144. 'Popular piety did not want a paradox but a 'miracle'. By this kind of piety the way for every possible superstition was opened.'

84 For discussion of the virgin birth, see Dunn 1980; also Brown 1977, and Marshall 1978. The remark of the last mentioned (p. 76), 'From the historical point of view acceptance of the virgin birth is not unreasonable granted the possibility of the Incarnation', represents an understanding of God's relationship to this world diametrically opposed to the one I have proposed. Cf. Williams 1985, 200.

85 It is not suggested here that God is not encountered except where the name of Jesus Christ is known. See p. 65.

86 Since 'sinlessness' has personal connotations inapplicable to a book, the widespread but tragically misguided transference of ultimacy to the Bible (instead of Jesus) is by the same logic expressed in terms of inerrancy. See Williams 1985, 286.

6

FAITHS IN THE LIGHT OF THE CHRISTIAN FAITH [1]

The relationship of Christianity to other faiths has become a matter of increasing concern both theologically and politically in our pluralist society. The basic problem facing Christians is this. Traditionally they have believed and taught that saving knowledge of God comes through Jesus Christ, who is uniquely divine and human, the second person of the Trinity incarnate. Such a claim to Christ's ultimacy is liable to offend on three counts. First, adherents of other faiths will object to being relegated to an inferior status. Secondly (and a related point), it may be feared that such an attitude will harm community relations and even lead to violence. Thirdly, many Christians would think it was contrary to God's love and justice revealed in Christ that the great majority of human beings who had never heard of him or had the chance to hear of him, should be denied knowledge of God or the hope of salvation. Simply to say with Augustine that they all sinned in Adam and so deserve condemnation[2] seems incompatible with the love and righteousness of God. If on the other hand it is argued that the loving God must have opened the ways to salvation to the rest of humanity, it becomes difficult to maintain Christian belief in the ultimacy of Jesus.

Before engaging with the problem, it is important to note that there are underlying assumptions that will influence reactions to this issue, such as relate to the authority of scripture, creeds, tradition, the Church, the way religious language functions, and the influence of the historical and cultural situation in which it is employed.

The relation of the Christian faith to other faiths is commonly discussed under three headings. This is liable to oversimplify a complex situation and obscure significant differences. Nevertheless, the headings, exclusivist,

Chapter 6

inclusivist, and pluralist,³ can serve to identify three broadly distinguishable positions from which to explore the issues:

a. Exclusivist

First we have the exclusivist position, held by some Protestants and some Roman Catholics (especially before the second Vatican Council). To defend it, evangelicals are likely to appeal to scripture, for example, to John 14:6, which reads, 'Jesus said to him "1 am the way, the truth, and the life, no one comes to the Father, except through me"' or to Acts 4:12, in Peter's speech referring to Jesus Christ, 'There is salvation in no one else, for there is no other name under heaven given among mortals by which we must be saved.' Roman Catholics or Anglo-Catholics might also appeal to tradition, perhaps going back to Cyprian, bishop of Carthage (martyred in AD 258), whose position can be summed up in the ancient axiom, '*Extra ecclesiam nulla salus est*' ('outside the Church there is no salvation'). This exclusivist view was expressed in extreme terms at the Council of Florence in 1445 as follows: 'No one remaining outside the Catholic Church, not just pagans, but also Jews or heretics or schismatics, can become partakers of eternal life; but they will go to the everlasting fire prepared for the devil and his angels, unless before the end of life they are joined to the Church'.⁴

Equally unaccommodating on the Protestant side was the declaration of the Congress on World Mission at Chicago in 1960,⁵ which declared: 'In the years since the war, more than one billion souls have passed into eternity and more than half of these went to the torment of hell fire without even hearing of Jesus Christ, who He was, or why He died on the cross of Calvary'. These two quotations focus on the ultimate destiny of human beings, heaven or hell, and not just on whether God is encountered apart from Christ in the present.

Someone who is less dogmatic about the next world, but equally uncompromising about this is the Swiss theologian Karl Barth. Shortly before the outset of the First World War he reacted vehemently against the nineteenth-century liberal theology he had been brought up on. As he saw it, it placed so much emphasis on subjective experience of God, that is, on God encountered in the human spirit, that one might say that it risked mistaking the human spirit for God. In 1914 Barth was aghast to see his theology teachers among the ninety three intellectuals, led by von Harnack, who signed a manifesto in support of the Kaiser's war policy. Not just the human spirit, but the German spirit, seemed to be mistaken for God. So what was good for Germany was thought to be good for God,

Faiths in the light of the Christian Faith

and vice versa. Barth reacted with prophetic outrage: God is wholly other, not the human spirit, which is totally corrupt and fallen and incapable of finding or knowing God apart from his self-revelation in Christ and with the aid of the Holy Spirit. Thus he concludes that religion is unbelief,[6] and that all religions are as much use as the tower of Babel, simply futile man-made attempts to reach God. The only valid revelation is God's revelation of himself in Christ.

It helps to see Barth in context. Even those who think he went over the top can recognize that his protest was necessary, not only against the Kaiser, but even more so against Hitler, and against the German Christians who supported Hitler, such as the theologian Emmanuel Hirsch, who even went so far as to say that Hitler was the voice of God to the German people.[7]

But Barth had more to offer than simply a prophetic protest. In the first place he made a very powerful case for the exclusiveness of Christian epistemology, that is, for a specifically Christian understanding of theological language. To take an example, the word 'sin' can mean different things to different people. The Jews took sin very seriously precisely because they took God so seriously. They understood sin in the light of God's law given to Moses. Those who loved God would gladly keep his commandments (as is movingly illustrated in Psalm 119). Anyone who did not so love and obey, or who in any way seemed to question or to undermine the Law of Moses, was liable to be seen as an enemy of God, a sinner by definition, who had to be dealt with. And so it would seem to some at least that Jesus had to be dealt with as a sinner and blasphemer (see p. 43 above).

However, Jesus' followers were convinced that he was right with God, and not a sinner, but, on the contrary, the very criterion of righteousness. On that assumption those who crucified Jesus were judged to be the sinners. There was no need to check this view in a dictionary of sin; that would have been absurd. In the light of faith, Jesus was the norm of righteousness in contrast to sin, and revealed the truth in relation to every aspect of God's relationship to humanity. This at its simplest is Barth's position. Those who are in faith, by God's grace, discern truth and righteousness in Christ and do not need to check their conclusions against any other source of knowledge, whether philosophy, or Natural Theology, or the Law of Moses, or any other religious views, or whatever. Any such cross-checking would imply that Jesus was not the ultimate norm in the first place.

This is, I think, Barth's strength. He makes it clear that Christians arrive at their understanding and knowledge not only of sin, but of God, through Jesus Christ. To relate to God in the light of Christ is what it is to be a Christian. But Barth draws a further conclusion, that those who do not know God in Christ, not only have no knowledge of God[8] and no living relationship with him, but are nevertheless, despite their ignorance, somehow guilty of rebellion against God and blameworthy for their predicament. In their fallen state human beings cannot even diagnose the problem properly, let alone arrive anywhere near the solution. It is like having stomach pain and supposing I have indigestion when I have cancer. I am right to suppose there is a problem; but I am nowhere near a solution without professional divine assistance. It is at this point that some may wonder if Barth has overstated his case.[9] Ironically, though he is so keen to defend God's freedom, he seems to restrict the freedom of the Holy Spirit. Its role is so narrowly restricted to the task of communicating God's self-revelation in Christ as to deny the freedom of God in the Spirit to be present anywhere in his creation, not least with his human creation.

However, though Barth would exclude any true revelatory or salvific value from other religions, he would not exclude anyone from heaven. To put it more cautiously, he was convinced that just as the Fall had embraced the whole of humanity, so now the saving work of Christ embraced the whole of humanity. Faced with the charge of universalism, he did not presume to lay down what God must do, but retorted with three observations, that there was no need to panic over the word [universalism], that Colossians 1:19[10] should be taken seriously, and anyway 'what of the 'danger' of the eternally skeptical, critical theologian who is ever and again suspiciously questioning, because fundamentally always legalistic and therefore in the main morosely gloomy?...This much is certain, that we have no theological right to set any sort of limits to the loving-kindness of God which has appeared in Jesus Christ'.[11] It follows that Barth should not be counted as an exclusivist without qualification. He excludes knowledge of God apart from Christ, but he does not exclude humanity at large from salvation.

Despite the generosity of spirit seen above, Barth would seem to many today to be too dismissive of the value of other religions in this world. However, his views illustrate the need to take care over using such labels as 'exclusivism'. One needs to ask, exclusion of or from what?

If the generalization can be allowed, it would seem that exclusivism is the corollary of attaching great weight to the Fall and the seriousness of sin and hence on the importance of Christ as the only saviour. In contrast, pluralists would seem to attach less weight to sin and the Fall and to put more emphasis on Christ as illuminator or channel of grace, but not necessarily the only one.

b. Inclusivist

The label 'inclusivist' signifies those who acknowledge Jesus to be the definitive revelation of God, in the light of which truth may be discerned discriminatingly in other faiths; and we may suppose these other faiths to have, not only true knowledge, but saving truth and a living relationship in some sense with God. There are many variations on this theme, Roman Catholic and Protestant.

To take the Roman Catholic side first, Vatican II has been described as in effect repealing Cyprian's doctrine of *extra ecclesiam nulla salus est* by declaring that there is salvation outside the visible Church. Thus we read in *The Pastoral Constitution of the Church*, in a reference to Christ's redeeming sacrifice: 'All this holds true, not only for Christians, but for all men of goodwill in whose hearts grace works in an unseen way ... The Holy Spirit, in a manner known only to God, offers every man the possibility of being associated with this paschal mystery'.[12]

Pope John Paul II put it even more strongly in his first encyclical *Redemptor Hominis* in 1979: 'Man – every man without exception whatever – has been redeemed by Christ, ... because with man – with each man without any exception whatever – Christ is in a way united, even when man is unaware of it.'[13]

The Vatican II declaration *Nostra Aetate* states: 'The Catholic Church rejects nothing which is holy and true in these religions.'[14]

However, in the Dogmatic Constitution of the Church (*Lumen Gentium*) it is made clear that: 'Whatever goodness or truth is found among them is looked upon by the Church as preparation for the Gospel', and in the Decree on Missionary Activity (*Ad Gentes*) we read: 'All must be converted to [Christ] as He is made known by the Church's preaching. All must be incorporated into him by baptism, and into the Church which is His body.'[15]

Vatican II drew heavily on the work of the theologian Karl Rahner, who coined the phrase 'anonymous Christians'. Without mentioning Barth, he explicitly rejects Barth's views: 'We must rid ourselves of the prejudice that we can face non-Christian religion with the dilemma that it must either come from God in everything it contains ..., or be simply a purely human construction.'[16] On the contrary, Rahner holds that every man can have a genuine saving relationship to God in his particular religion and that 'it would be wrong to regard the pagan as someone who has not yet been touched in any way by God's grace and truth.'[17]

Rahner sees an analogy to the status of other faiths in the case of Old

Testament religion before Christ. Just as Christ is the true destination of Old Testament religion, so he is for all religion; and it is the Church's duty to bring all to a conscious recognition of Christ. This is the point at which the anonymous Christian discovers the full truth of what he has before known only in part and without the name of Christ. Exactly when the genuine existential encounter occurs cannot be judged externally; but it does matter if someone meets Christ and rejects him.

Hans Küng criticised Rahner's theory as the most recent 'theological fabrication' attempting to sweep 'the whole of good-willed humanity' into the backdoor of the Holy Roman Church leaving no one of goodwill "outside", and in the process to save the formula 'outside the Church no salvation'.[18] Küng urges the abandonment of that dogma and of the formula 'anonymous Christian'. He advocates instead distinguishing between the 'ordinary' way of salvation in the world religions and the 'extraordinary' way in the Church. He writes: 'A man is to be saved within the religion that is made available to him in his historical situation. Hence it is his right and duty to seek God within that religion in which the hidden God has already found him ... the 'ordinary' way of salvation, as against which the way of salvation in the Church appears as something very special and extraordinary.'[19] But then it turns out that the ordinary way is only an interim measure till explicit Christian faith is arrived at. In his later work Küng has moved towards a pluralist position (see below).

On the Protestant side mention must be made of Paul Tillich, a contemporary of Barth. Tillich had the distinction of being on the first list of non-Jewish German theologians to be sacked by Hitler in 1933 because of his outspoken condemnation of Nazism. He was offered a post in Union Theological Seminary in New York and only just got away in time, though reluctant to leave Germany. His theology was very influential in the United States in the 1950s and 1960s and hit the British public in the guise of John Robinson's book, *Honest to God*.[20]

Tillich agreed with Barth that there was no salvation without revelation and vice versa;[21] but whereas Barth concluded there was no revelation and therefore no salvation outside Christianity,[22] Tillich saw the signs of salvation outside Christianity and therefore evidence of revelation, that is, of saving grace, of the 'New Being'[23] at work in other communities of faith. Like Rahner he therefore concluded that God was revealing himself in saving power in other faiths. Tillich took 'salvation' to mean 'healing' (from the Latin *salvare*). Any work of healing had to be the work of God, not the devil or Beelzebub (Mark 3:22). But for Tillich, Jesus as the Christ,

Faiths in the light of the Christian Faith

the bearer of New Being, was the norm and criterion of health. Jesus was the supreme manifestation of the power to overcome every destructive manifestation of human fallenness or estrangement.

So although Tillich had a very positive attitude towards other faiths, he held Christ to be definitive and ultimate. Christians should therefore be ready to listen to other faiths and to learn from them, and perhaps to discover God in unexpected ways and places.[24] But Tillich also recognized that all religions, including Christianity, could go wrong; as he wrote '*Falsa religio* is not identical with special historical religions but with the self-saving attempts in every religion, even in Christianity.'[25] It occurs when something less than God is mistaken for God himself, when the penultimate is treated as the ultimate; another word for that is idolatry.[26] The outcome of treating what may be good in itself as *ultimate* is to render it demonic with destructive consequences. The significance of Christ and his cross lies in his power to overcome every kind of demonic idolatry. I will be coming back to that.

c. Pluralist

First, the Pluralist view will be considered briefly here, not because it lacks importance, but because the principle of it is basically simple, namely that God is at work and revealed in all religions; Christianity is but one way of salvation among others. This view is closely associated with John Hick and his call for a 'Copernican revolution' (see below). On his appointment as Professor of Theology at Birmingham University Hick became involved in community and race relations work. He met Muslims, Sikhs, and Hindus, as well as Jews, and was astonished at the signs of godliness they showed. (One might think here of Jesus' astonishment at the unexpected faith of the Roman centurion: Luke 7:9). This could hardly be explained as the spin-off of Christianity in Birmingham. Was it then of Beelzebub? (cf. Mark 3:22). To think so would be blasphemous! It could only be what these people claimed, the fruit of their own faiths. In *God Has Many Names* Hick writes of:

> Human beings opening their minds to a higher divine Reality, known as personal and good and as demanding righteousness and love between man and man ... Without ever being tempted to become either a Hindu or a Buddhist, I could see that within these ancient religions men and women are savingly related to the Eternal Reality from which we all live.[27]

This experience and his reading of Wilfred Cantwell Smith's book, *The Meaning and End of Religion*,[28] led Hick to propose a 'Copernican

Revolution' in the theology of religions. By that he meant: 'A shift from a Christianity-centred or Jesus-centred to a God-centred model of the universe of Faiths. One then sees the great world religions as different human responses to the one divine Reality, embodying different perceptions which have been formed in different historical and cultural circumstances.'[29]

Hick recognized that this meant reopening the Christological question and of course the doctrine of the Trinity, because if Jesus was literally the second person of the Trinity incarnate, Christianity's claims would remain unique and one could not affirm the equal value of other faiths. But if that language could be understood as the metaphorical,[30] or mythological, or poetic expression of the Christian's devotion to his Lord, the implications of a literal understanding could be avoided. However, it needs to be said here that it is possible to treat Christian language about God and Christ as symbolic without necessarily being forced to accept Hick's 'Copernican revolution', or having to conclude that Jesus is only another prophet.

This brings us to the problems posed by the different viewpoints. Two of the most serious were mentioned at the start. A critique of each position that has been outlined above is implicit in the other two. So the problems can be stated briefly.

a. The **exclusivist** view poses an acute problem for belief in God's love and justice. Quite apart from that, in our pluralist society, not to mention the world's global village, it seems to show contempt for other faiths, which bodes ill for race and community relations in Britain or any other country. Even as it purports to offer a Gospel of peace and reconciliation, exclusivist Christianity may seem more likely to provoke an uncompromising conflict between different claims to truth, justified by appeal to God. All the same, it does at least uphold the traditional claims for Christ's uniqueness and God's saving intervention in Him. The question is whether this is the only way in which this message can be maintained? The underlying concern, the hidden agenda, may perhaps be a desire to keep traditional interpretations of scripture and tradition unchanged, for fear that any change can only mean total collapse. Such fear may not be justified. One's judgement here will depend very much on one's view of scripture, and the high or low value that one puts on the critical study of scripture and tradition.

A very real danger exists of attributing to the written word of scripture (written in Greek, a human cultural creation), the ultimacy that according to the New Testament itself, belongs uniquely to Jesus Christ himself (see

John 20:21; Philippians 2:9 and indeed the whole of the New Testament). The ultimacy of Christ is expressed, as we have seen, in the attribution of sinlessness to him. The understandable but unjustifiable attribution of ultimacy to the primary *witness* to Christ is expressed in terms of the inerrancy of scripture.[31] This leads to demonic manifestations of fundamentalism, even where the sincere intention is to uphold the Christian faith.

The critical issue that arises here in the debate about Exclusivism is whether exclusion is determined by the written words of scripture – certain proof texts – or by the vision of God in Christ arising out of the totality of his life and death as portrayed in scripture. If this is ultimate, then other visions of God, however rich and noble in themselves, nevertheless take second place. A similar question arises over tradition and the danger of attributing ultimacy to the Church's witness (or to its spokesmen) at the expense of the one they witness to.

b. The charge against **Inclusivism** from the 'right wing' is that it is already watering down the uniqueness of Christ and the saving significance of his death. The 'left wing' on the other hand, see it as a patronizing extension of the exclusivist view, involving complicated modifications which Hick likens to pre-Copernican 'epicycles' because 'they are so powerfully reminiscent of the epicycles that were added to the old Ptolemaic picture of the universe to accommodate increasingly accurate knowledge of the planets.'[32]

Hick gives as an example of a theological 'epicycle' the pronouncement of Pius IX as long ago as 1854, who stood by the *extra ecclesiam* dogma, but added that 'those who are affected by ignorance of true religion, if it is invincible ignorance, are not subject to any guilt in this matter before the eyes of the Lord.'[33] A paradoxical implication of Pius IX's doctrine might be that missionaries are liable to send many more people to hell than to heaven. The 'invincibly ignorant' in Africa or Asia, or this country for that matter, have a chance of heaven; but if they hear the Gospel and don't respond, they are doomed to hell! So Hick and others these days reject the 'epicycles' of Pius or Rahner or Tillich, and advocate instead the pluralist view in order to meet objections to the other views, to defend God's love and justice, and to affirm non-Christian faiths and their adherents.

c. However, **Pluralism** has problems of its own, apart from its acknowledged departure from traditional Christian faith in the uniqueness

Chapter 6

and ultimacy of Christ. It advocates religious co-existence and mutual respect, which is admirable in its way, but not as simple as it looks. Here one can make three distinctions as between 'mystical co-existence', 'moral co-existence', and, for want of a better word, 'futurist co-existence'. It is relatively easy to point to close parallels in the language of worship to God, 'Supreme Lord, to whom we humble creatures bow in adoration and whom we cannot adequately describe', and so on. Any theist could use such phrases, and there does indeed seem to be much common ground in Church, Synagogue, Temple, Gudwara, or Mosque. A sense of shared, mystical experience within the context of prayer and worship is certainly not to be decried, but outside that circle things get harder.

Moral and practical decisions have to be taken which may be mutually exclusive, as has arisen in the Christian churches over the issues of homosexuality, the ordination of women, and the consecration of bishops. Similarly, one cannot treat some people as untouchable and at the same time proclaim all to be equal as children of God and fallen sinners. Hick rightly takes Christians to task for comparing their supposed virtues with the vices of others; and Christianity's record has indeed been terrible with the crusades and inquisition, etc. But the point here is simply that discrimination is necessary. Hick knows this and tries to establish principles for it; but this might seem no less patronizing than appealing directly to what we know of Jesus, in order to discern what is godly or ungodly. That indeed is where Hick started from, but now he seems to make his own judgement the criterion of truth.

Thirdly, the problem of 'futurist co-existence' arises. In short, what will Hinduism, Islam, Sikhism, Judaism or Christianity be like in ten or fifty years time? None can be everything at once. To take some topical illustration, the Church of England will in ten years time be a Church which either does or does not appoint women to be bishops, or admit practising gays to the priesthood; or it may split completely in half over these issues, but it cannot be everything at once.

There are inescapable limits to co-existence advocated by Pluralists, even if every effort is made to be peaceful. The co-existence of faiths may be more easily achieved in the context of mystical co-existence amongst individuals, but much harder in relation to moral or futurist co-existence or where divergent communities are involved. It is interesting here to note that the exclusivist position ties in with an emphasis on life in this world and on the importance of history, as is the case with Judaism, Christianity, Islam (and Marxism viewed as a quasi-religion).

Faiths in the light of the Christian Faith

A further criticism of the pluralist view is that pluralists tend to reduce religion to a cultural phenomenon. To an extent that is what it is, and on a cultural level we can accept pluralism. Although deep down we may find it hard to accept, yet in our rational moments we admit that the French are entitled to be French, or even the Amerindians Amerindian, without being required to become English. But as I have argued above (p. 2), I question whether religion can rightly be reduced completely to a cultural phenomenon. It is the context in which ultimate questions are raised and attempts are made to answer them. The answers may be wrong or inadequate; but at least that is the issue. Hick speaks of 'the Eternal Reality from which we all live',[34] but leaves this reality totally hidden, as it were, behind cultural manifestations. God in that case seems to be so hidden that we cannot talk about him, or at least make any truth claims at all; and religion is denied the right to its proper subject matter. Or worse, if we accept that religions are trying to talk about the ultimate, and we regard very different or even contradictory accounts as equally valid, then I fear that we run the risk of theological apartheid!

This isn't entirely fair to Pluralism; but if in effect one says: 'What is ultimately true for me is not ultimately true for you', it might suggest that we are two different species, for whom separate development is appropriate, and for whom salvation ultimately means different things. In other words, there is a danger in pluralism of 'cryptopolytheism', and the loss not only of the reality of one God, but of the reality of one humanity, a final surrender to the fragmentation of postmodernism.

After this brief exploration of the issues, we can consider what conclusions may be drawn. In chapter 1 I took issue with the notion that all the various possible understandings and manifestations of human personhood or selfhood are equally valid, and just part of the rich variety of life. In part they are, with the different possibilities they offer of actualizing the potential of human personhood; but some to a greater or lesser extent block the realization of that potential. In the same way I would like to take issue with the view that every understanding of God is equally valid and simply part of the rich variety of human religious life.

We can accept that different answers to the ultimate questions may, in different ways and to a different extent, open the door for human beings to reach towards God, and for God to reach towards them. But I believe that some understandings of God and the human response demanded by them are detrimental to the fulfilling of human life, more or less so. For me as a Christian, the criterion of judgement (meaning not condemnation

Chapter 6

but critical appreciation) is not and should not be merely my opinion, but that vision of a personal, ultimate reality which comes to us through Jesus Christ, that is, from the reality whom he called Father, for which or rather whom the indispensable source for us now is the New Testament. It witnesses to, but is not identical with, the Eternal Reality from which and to which we all live, the true source and goal of individual, corporate, cultural, human life, in relationship to whom human beings become persons.

It remains the case that human beings may actualize their potential as persons in varying degrees and in an almost infinite number of ways, from ballet dancer to weight lifter, from businessman to social worker. Similar diversity can be seen and welcomed in the coming to be of persons in the context of different cultures and nations, and finally in the different manifestations of the spiritual dimension of human life, in short, in the diversity of religions. Here the danger is not of diversity of religions as such, but of claims to ultimacy for what is not truly ultimate within them.

To conclude then. It is indeed a mistake for any limited partial account or description of the ultimate reality (God) to be treated as the whole truth. We're not there yet; we haven't reached the goal. We live in faith and hope, not with complete knowledge. So Barth is right to recognize the danger when the human spirit-in-the-making mistakes itself for the divine creative spirit. Tillich is equally right to see this danger of idolatry with its demonic consequences. But Barth is wrong, I think, when he restricts the Holy Spirit to the role of enlightening and enlivening only those to whom the Christian Gospel is preached. The power of person-making is at work in every human community. So Tillich, I think, is right in opposition to Barth in seeing the power of New Being at work in all humanity. In my terms, the person-creating power of God is present with, and available to, every human being created in the image of the true Person and capable of growing into the reality of personhood. But no one can be blind to the obstructions and corruptions facing the project of personhood, and put in its way by individuals, communities, cultures, even in some sense by the natural world, and not least by religions as they function in the world.

The question then arises not only of creating but of recreating persons, not only of advancing, but of liberating the trapped, not only of flourishing, but of healing the wounded and injured and fallen. So finally, with Tillich again, I would hold that Christianity is not so much a religion of revelation as a religion of healing, or rather, of revelation in and through the power of healing. What is needed is not only the healing and redemption and

Faiths in the light of the Christian Faith

salvation of individuals, but the healing and redemption of religions if they are to be the means of salvation.

In short, the question really is not so much whether we can adequately describe the mysterious other we call God. The question is how any and every inadequate concept of humanity and of God which inhibits or corrupts human potentiality can be overcome, so that the way to personhood is open again, and the path cleared towards becoming what from our infancy, even if subconsciously, we yearned to be – truly person, loving and loved in the community of persons and of the personal God who intends that goal. Jesus confronts us as truly person and as the creator of persons through his selfgiving love.

It is on the cross that we discover what person-making power really is; it is not like any exercise of worldly power (cf. Luke 22:24–27). Here Barth is right again: as Christians we discover the truth in Jesus Christ. In the light of Jesus we arrive at our understanding of the words 'humanity' and 'God', or as I would prefer to put it, what we mean by human person, and what we mean by divine person. This is something to be shared with others who are by no means totally ignorant of what we are talking about. Rahner and Tillich are right here against Barth, I think; human beings do already have something of what they want to be given. And though I do not agree with everything Pope John Paul II may say, maybe he is right too when he says, as I quoted above: 'With man – with each man without any exception whatever – Christ is in a way united, even when man is unaware of it' (meaning, of course, every man and woman, every human person).[35]

So finally, Pluralism has an obvious place at the cultural level in general. It also has a place at the cultural level within religions. We should have no difficulty with that idea within Christianity, where we can see the amazing degree of pluralism – of diversity – among members of every Church and not least within the Anglican Church. We should certainly meet and talk and listen together and be prepared to be astonished at the possibilities of godliness actualized not only in Christian congregations and traditions that are very different from our own, but within the great religions of the world.[36]

Beyond that, I also believe that there is room to acknowledge a kind of pluralism among the world's religions, and not merely at the cultural level. We are simply not treating them seriously as religions if we do not recognize that they raise and respond to questions of ultimacy. Within the diversity of answers offered, Christians who have the courage to engage in serious dialogue with those of other religions, may be astonished yet again to discover God at work in unexpected places and in unexpected ways. From this they can learn something more of the power of person-making and the potential of personhood. But if there is an encompassing truth for humanity in its totality, an ultimate goal for which human beings yearn, then perhaps it is not inconceivable that it should have come to light in a genuinely human personal life. Those who know that life, and whose own lives are informed, infused, and healed by it, may dare to believe that they have actually been given something of supreme worth which they should share with the whole of humanity inclusively. At the heart of it all is a love willing to sacrifice itself to give life to others. If that is ultimate, nothing else can be.

Notes

1 The original version of this chapter was a paper given at a consultation on 'Exploration of Beliefs', March 1991, at St Georges, Windsor.

2 *Opus imperfectum contra Julianum*, 6.22.

3 As in D'Costa 1986.

4 Quoted by Hick 1980, 49.

5 Ibid., 49.

6 Barth 1936, 299 f. Cf. Zahrnt 1965, 34 for a summary of Barth's vivid and vehement critique of religion, drawn from his *Epistle to the Romans* (transln, London, 1933).

7 See Ericksen 1985, 148.

8 This may be qualified by Barth's admission of 'secular parables', but their elements of truth could still only be recognised from the standpoint of revelation in Christ. See Hunsinger 2000, 334 f.

9 For other examples of the exclusivist position, *viz*. Kraemer, Brunner, Newbigin, see Race 1993.

10 Col. 1:20 '... and through him God was pleased to reconcile to himself all things, whether on earth or in heaven, by making peace through the blood of his cross'.

11 Barth 1961, 59 f.

12 Flannery (ed.) 1988, 924.

13 *Redemptor Hominis* (London: Catholic Truth Society, 1979) para. 14. Quoted in Hick and Knitter (eds.) 1988, 21.

14 Ibid., 21

15 Ibid., 21

16 Rahner 1966, 127, quoted by D'Costa 1986, 87.

17 Quote in Hick and Hebblethwaite (eds.) 1980, 75.

18 Küng 1976, 98.

Faiths in the light of the Christian Faith

19 Quoted in Hick 1973, 128.
20 Robinson 1963.
21 See Tillich 1978, i. 144 f. And ii. 166 f.
22 Other than through the all encompassing work of Christ, see p. 140 above.
23 For the important concept of the New Being see Tillich 1978, i. 49 f. and ii. 118 ff.
24 See Tillich 1963.
25 Tillich 1978, ii. 86.
26 Op. cit., i. 13. See also p. 2 and 63 above.
27 Op. cit., 5.
28 Cantwell Smith 1962.
29 Hick 1980, 5 f.
30 See Hick 1993, ch. 10.
31 See ch. 5 n. 86 above.
32 Hick 1973, 124.
33 Quoted in Hick, op. cit., 123.
34 Hick 1980, 5.
35 See n. 13 above.
36 A discovery which had such an impact on Hick. See Hick 1980, 7.

7

CONCLUSION

The situation is really very simple. Is it worth living for what Jesus was willing to die for? Might it even be worth dying for what he was willing to live for? It's possible to say 'No' and to set Jesus aside as little more than a misguided idealist who came to a tragic end. It's also possible to say 'I don't know', which may well be honest but in effect is to set Jesus at arms length among the many other 'don't knows' that we carry around with us every day as we try to cope with the busy-ness of life. Finally it is also possible to say 'Yes' and in doing so to acknowledge his ultimacy and to accept the consequences (cf. Mark 8:34)

This I believe can be a conscious decision which anyone can take, (if they dare!) but which too many are reluctant to do so, perhaps for fear of denying the primacy of grace and falling into the heresy of Pelagius (see p. 29, n. 42). But this may result in a tendency to hang around evading the issue and waiting for a Damascus road experience to override our normal earthly conditions and responsibilities. But such an experience as St Paul's is the privilege of a very few (for which they can be truly grateful). For others it is or should be a simple matter of recognizing a challenging possibility and going for it, without the benefits of proof, but with the benefit of Scripture and the examples of Jesus-shaped lives in history and in our world today, and above all with the prospect of finding meaning and direction, healing and hope in their lives.

We should not be afraid of seeing Jesus as the supreme example of being human. We are very familiar these days with the importance of role models. Celebrities in sport and elsewhere are constantly called upon to recognize their responsibilities as role models. Rarely if ever do we hear it debated whether there should be role models let alone whether the very idea is a delusion. They are rather to be regarded as ways of being and behaving which are good in themselves and which are offered to others for their

Chapter 7

own and society's good. But it is still up to others to accept for themselves the model offered to them, or to reject it. What is at stake is not just one example among others but the definitive disclosure of what it is to be human and divine.

Whoever accepts the ultimacy of Jesus, the vision of life, of love and of justice, that meets us in his story, has certainly taken a tremendous challenge on themselves. They shouldn't be compelled take up *unnecessary* additional burdens and demands as a condition of following Jesus, such as having to believe what is today impossible to believe in the light of advances in science. If unnecessary obstacles to faith and commitment can be cleared away, the opponents of Christianity might at least begin to face up to the reality of what they reject; they might even be ready at last to answer the question, In the name of whom or what do you reject the ultimacy of Jesus? However, I suspect that if the path was cleared, many secularists would be greatly heartened and ready to follow it wherever it led, and to face up to the real challenge posed by the ultimacy of Jesus.

Appendix

THE DOCTINE OF THE TRINITY AS THE FOUNDATION OF THE CHRISTIAN FAITH[1]

Readings: Joshua 1:1–9; Matthew 28:16–20

The doctrine of the Trinity remains the touchstone of orthodoxy for the main Christian Churches, and the feast of the Holy Trinity is the crown of the Church's year. It celebrates the climax of God's self-revelation as Father, Son and Holy Spirit. Yet for a great many people it is not only as incomprehensible as the Athanasian Creed[2] disarmingly acknowledges, but also irrelevant to ordinary life. However, as Chaplain of a college dedicated to the Holy and Undivided Trinity, I hope it will seem appropriate for me to address this theme, especially on Trinity Sunday.

It is my conviction that far from being incomprehensible and irrelevant, the doctrine of the Trinity is basically comprehensible and profoundly relevant to everyday life, and far too important to be left to professional theologians.

I would like to approach this theme from the ground upwards, so to speak, rather than from heaven or from heavenly revelation downwards. It has to do with the question of God and, of course, there's no denying the ultimate mystery of God's being, but my immediate concern is not with the being of God but with the question of God – a question that is hard to avoid, whatever answers people may give to it.

The question is basically whether life has any ultimate meaning, depth or purpose? or is human life simply a flash in the evolutionary pan, a transient anomaly thrown up by an incomprehensible cosmic bang? No one can impose their answers on anybody else, but to say 'yes' to an ultimate meaning and purpose is to say 'yes', at least implicitly, to the reality of God. And that's where the trouble starts because of the almost infinite number of ways in which that 'yes' can be interpreted or envisaged. And this matters because if God is by definition the true ground and goal of all things, then that includes ourselves. So to be right about God is to be right about ourselves, and to get God wrong would be to get ourselves wrong. The key question then is: Where or how can we arrive at the truth of God and of ourselves?

Innumerable answers, as I say, have been offered in history and still surround us and compete for our attention. The one I want to propose is the belief that there is an ultimate reality, God, who is personal, and who reveals himself and relates to us as persons. Our understanding of personal relationships must, therefore, in some measure have a bearing on the relationships between God and humanity. So I need to say a brief word about them.

Personal relationships involve two kinds of knowing, a knowing about, which can be put into words and shared; and a knowing which is nearer to loving, which is open to the future, the as yet unknown but not empty future – rather one full of promise. This knowing can never be put fully into words, but is certainly no less real for all that. For simplicity, we may speak of the objective and subjective aspects of personal knowing, and if God is personal, knowledge of God must involve a knowing about and a deeper intimate knowing of God.

Knowledge of persons is not something we can take hold of from outside; it depends on persons being willing to open themselves up to each other, as we say. So knowing God, we may suppose, will depend on his being willing to open himself up, to make himself known, and to reveal himself by giving knowledge about himself, objectively, yet within the intimacy of relationship, subjectively.

These two aspects belong together. Dangers arise when they are forced apart or one is over emphasized at the expense of the other. At the extremes lie the dangers of tyranny or anarchy – the tyranny of objective revelation arises when all the emphasis is put on objectively known facts about God, supposedly revealed and binding for ever, at the expense of openness to new discovery within a loving relationship.

At the opposite extreme we find the anarchy of subjective revelation, the claim to an intimate personal knowing of God not subject to any rule or shared knowledge about God., in short, an arbitrary claim supported by unsupportable claims to inspiration by the Spirit.

I now want to narrow my scope still further and to turn to a particular community which believed that a personal God had opened himself up and made himself and his purposes known within an intimate, loving relationship. In the Old Testament we find both aspects of knowing God, sometimes in tension, sometimes in harmony. The harmony is beautifully expressed in Psalm 119. The love of God is found in a relationship defined by the Law of Moses. 'Lord, what love have I unto thy law, all the day long is my study in it' (verse 97). This Psalm alone refutes the charge of arid legalism too often made by Christians against the Judaism of Jesus' day. It and many other Psalms witness to a community defined by its commitment to the Law of Moses, open to a living, loving relationship with God.

The foundational terms of this relationship are spelled out explicitly in Joshua 1:5–9, 'Moses my servant is dead. As I was with Moses, so I will be with you', – the promise of an ongoing, living, loving relationship – 'so long as you are careful to do all the Law my servant Moses commanded you'; – the Law delivered, according to the tradition, on Mount Sinai.

Here we see a clear Trinitarian structure of relationship with God. God the transcendent source and goal of all things is believed to have made his will and purposes known objectively in the Law of Moses, the Torah, while his living presence is promised, as it were subjectively, to those who live according to his revealed will.

Against this background, the strikingly similar structure of the concluding words of Matthew's Gospel stands out clearly. I take these words to be expressing the author's faith, rather than recording Jesus' *ipsissima verba*. But the point is the same either way. Jesus appears on the mountain, symbolic of Mount Sinai. The hint is confirmed by the words, 'All authority in heaven and on earth has been given to me'. This stupendous claim raises Jesus above the authority of the Law of Moses. Yet within Judaism, the Law had itself already been identified with the pre-existent wisdom of God, as in Ecclesiasticus 24:23. Referring to heavenly Wisdom, the author writes, 'All this is the book of the covenant of the covenant of the Most High God, the Law that Moses commanded us as an inheritance for the congregation of Jacob'. So to be above the Law was to be virtually, indeed actually, equal with God himself, hence, 'All authority in heaven and on earth.' Thus God is now seen to be revealed objectively, not in the Law, not in a book, but in a human person. One of Jesus' greatest achievements was not to write a book! He witnessed to God in his person.

Implicit in a claim to divine authority is a claim to universal truth. The ultimate must be universal. Thus Jesus is seen as the ultimate truth of God and humanity, the truth of all bodied out in history. The command follows naturally, 'Go therefore, and make disciples of all nations' (not just the Jews), baptizing them in the name of the Father, the Son (superseding the

Appendix

Law of Moses), and of the Holy Spirit.' The locus of objective revelation, of the truth *about* God, has shifted from the Law, the Torah, to Jesus, with radical consequences. A new community is constituted; its relationship to God is defined and informed by Jesus of Nazareth, his life and death, and all that that must mean; while it remains open to the future in a living, loving relationship, as we read, 'And lo, I am with you always to the close of the age.' Those simple words are Matthew's Pentecost.

Quite simply, this trinitarian structure, God known about in the person of Jesus Christ and through his continuing intimate presence in the Holy Spirit,[3] defines the Christian Church. Working out the implications for our understanding is the task of theology, and the implications for how we should live is the task of Christian ethics.

The implications for our understanding of the very being of God are at once simple and yet wrapped in mystery. In the first place we may see self-differentiation within the Godhead as the necessary ontological precondition of God's self-revelation in Christ and the Holy Spirit – the ontological corollary of the confession 'Jesus Christ is Lord'. How it can be so and what it means for God in himself is the mystery which in terms of human understanding we can only approach at the edges and with deep humility, yet without commitment to God in self-differentiation, the ultimacy of Jesus, the claim that Jesus Christ is truly Lord, would be shattered.

Theologians down the years have attempted to probe more deeply and with more or less humility, into the mystery of the threefold being of God himself. Some modern exponents have emphasized the relationality of the being of God and have seen it as the clue to the essential relationality of human beings, in contrast to heightened individualism of our age, shaped by its idolatrous worship of consumerism and market forces.

Theological reflection on the inner being of the Godhead may have its place, but more important, I believe, is the trinitarian confession that God for us, that is for Christians, is God the Father, ground and goal of all things, and Jesus Christ his Son, Lord and Saviour; and Holy Spirit, his living presence.

This constitutes the Christian Church and commits it to proclaiming that what it believes to be true is true for all.

Perhaps I've said enough to show that the doctrine of the doctrine of the Trinity is not totally incomprehensible, and that it is relevant to life. But it not only has the positive role of constituting the Church, it has also a negative or defensive role of warding off what threatens the Church and indeed human life at large.

Trinity Sunday sermon

If Jesus is truly Lord and God, if he is ultimate, then ultimacy is denied to anyone or to anything else. All forms of fundamentalism, all attempts to ascribe ultimate, infinite, divine value and authority to what is finite, are ruled out. That must apply to books, persons, traditions and institutions, not least those found within the frame of Christianity. They may be necessary and life enhancing in the service of Christ as Lord, but treated as 'lords' in themselves, they become demonic idols, leading to disaster.

But is there a danger in ascribing ultimacy to that man Jesus? Maybe there would have been if he had set himself as ultimate in the way of false claimants to ultimacy, but he resisted that temptation and willingly accepted his own self-negation in death. In so doing, Jesus opened the way to a living relationship with God in the future, shaped and informed by his own unique past. Against tyranny and anarchy, the extremes of objective or subjective revelation, the way of creative yet ordered freedom is opened up, in relationship with the living God through Jesus Christ in the Spirit. This is in no way to imply that there can be no knowledge of God apart from Christ; but for Christians its value is to be seen in the light of Christ.

The Trinity for Christians is certainly not to be located primarily in three mysterious pre-existent spiritual beings essentially remote from the world we live in. It is to be encountered first in Jesus of Nazareth in his loving relationship with God the Father, to which scripture bears witness, and secondly in the witness not only of Scripture but of experience of the Spirit in the life of the believer.

The reality creates the Church. The doctrine expresses and protects the faith of the Church that God is real who meets us and redeems us in Jesus Christ and remains with us in the Spirit always, even to the close of the age. And so to God the Father, Son and Holy Spirit be glory now and evermore.

Amen

Notes

1 Preached at All Souls College, Oxford on Trinity Sunday, 10 June 2001.

2 Included in the Book of Common Prayer under the title *Quicunque Vult*.

3 Some exponents of the Trinitarian mystery have looked to the Holy Spirit as a way of establishing a feminine element in the Godhead.

SELECT BIBLIOGRAPHY

Ackroyd, P.R. and Evans, C.F. (eds.)
   1970   *The Cambridge History of the Bible*, vol. i, *From the Beginnings to Jerome*, Cambridge.

Armstrong, A.H.
   1957   *An Introduction to Ancient Philosophy*, 3rd edn, London.

Avis, P. (ed.)
   1993   *The Resurrection of Jesus Christ*, London.

Barnes, J.
   1982   *Aristotle*, Oxford.

Barrett, C.K.
   1978   *The Gospel according to St John*, 2nd edn, London.

Barth, K.
   1936   *Church Dogmatics*, vol. i, pt. ii, transln, Edinburgh.
   1961   *The Humanity of God*, London.

Barton, S. and Stanton, G.S. (eds.)
   1994   *Resurrection: Essays in honour of Leslie Houlden*, London.

Berger, P.L.
   1969   *The Social Reality of Religion*, London. Published in the USA as *The Sacred Canopy*, New York, 1967.

Brown, R.E.
   1977   *The Birth of the Messiah*, London.
   1979   *The Community of the Beloved Disciple*, London.

Bultmann, R.
   1953   *New Testament and Mythology*, in H.W. Bartsch and R.F. Fuller, *Kerygma and Myth: A theological debate*, London.

Cantwell Smith, W.
   1962   *The Meaning and End of Religion*, New York and London.

Carnley, P.
   1987   *The Structure of Resurrection Belief*, Oxford.

Chadwick, H.
   1967   *A History of the Early Church*, Harmondsworth.

Charles, R.H. (ed.)
   1913   *The Apocrypha and Pseudepigrapha of the Old Testament*, vol. ii, London.

Cupitt, D.
   1980   *Taking Leave of God*, London.

Bibliography

    1994   *After All – Religion without Alienation*, London.
Daly, R.J.
    1978   *The Origins of the Christian Doctrine of Sacrifice*, London.
D'Costa, G.
    1986   *Theology and Religious Pluralism*, Oxford.
Davis, S.T.
    1993   *Risen Indeed: Making sense of the Resurrection*, London.
Dillon, J.
    1977   *The Middle Platonists: A study of Platonism 80 BC to AD 220*, London.
Douglas, M.
    1970   *Natural Symbols: Explorations in Cosmology*, London.
Dunn, J.D.G.
    1980   *Christology in the Making: An inquiry into the origin of the Christian doctrine of the Incarnation*, London.
    1985   *The Evidence for Jesus*, London.
Ericksen, R.O.
    1985   *Theologians under Hitler*, Newhaven and London.
Filoramo, G.
    1990   *A History of Gnosticism*, Oxford.
Flannery, A. (ed.)
    1988   *Vatican Council II*, revd edn, Leominster.
Glover, J.
    1988   *The Philosophy and Psychology of Personal Identity*, London.
Grant, R.M.
    1971   *From Augustus to Constantine*, London.
Gregg, R.C. and Groh, D.E. (eds.)
    1981   *Early Arianism*, London.
Grillmeier, A.
    1975   *Christ in Christian Tradition*, vol. i, 2nd revd edn, London and Oxford.
Guthrie, W.K.C.
    1975   *A History of Greek Philosophy*, vol. iv: *Plato the Man and his Dialogues: Earlier period*, Cambridge.
    1978   *A History of Greek Philosophy*, vol. v: *The Later Plato and the Academy*, Cambridge.
    1981   *A History of Greek Philosophy*, vol. vi: *Aristotle: An encounter*, Cambridge.
Hardy, E.R. (ed.)
    1954   *The Christology of the Later Fathers*, London and Philadelphia.
Hare, R.M.
    1982   *Plato*, Oxford.
Harré, R.
    1984   *Personal Being*, Cambridge, Mass.

Harré, R. (ed.)
   1976   *Personality*, Oxford.
Harvey, A.E.
   1982   *Jesus and the Constraints of History*, London.
Harvey, V.
   1967   *The Historian and the Believer*, London.
Harwood, R.
   1998   *The Survival of the Self*, Aldershot, Hants.
Heidegger, M.
   1978   *Being and Time*, transln. J. Macquarrie and E. Robinson, Oxford.
Hengel, M.
   1974   *Judaism and Hellenism*, transln, London.
   1976   *Son of God*, transln., London.
   1981   *The Atonement*, transln, London.
Hick, J.
   1989   *An Interpretation of Religion*, London.
   1980   *God has Many Names*, London.
   1993   *The Metaphor of God Incarnate*, London.
   1973   *God and the Universe of Faiths*, London.
Hick, J. and Hebblethwaite, B. (eds.)
   1980   *Christianity and Other Religions*, Glasgow.
Hick, J. and Knitter, P.F. (eds.)
   1988   *The Myth of Christian Uniqueness*, London.
Houlden, J.L.
   1986   *Connections*, London.
Hunsinger, G.
   2000   *Disruptive Grace: Studies in the theology of Karl Barth*, Cambridge.
Jansz, J.
   1991   *Person, Self, and Moral Demands*, Leiden.
Kähler, M.
   1964   *The so-called Historical Jesus and the Historic, Biblical, Christ*, Philadelphia.
Kelly, J.N.D.
   1977   *Early Christian Doctrines*, 5th edn, London.
Kummel, W.G.
   1973   *The New Testament*, London.
Küng, H.
   1976   *On Being a Christian*, transln, Glasgow.
Lampe, G.W.H.
   1977   *God as Spirit*, The Bampton Lectures 1976, Oxford.
Lietzman, H.
   1950   *A History of the Early Church, from Augustine to Julian*, London.
Liddell, H.G. and Scott, R.
   1883   *A Greek-English Lexicon*, 7th edn, Oxford.

Bibliography

McFadyen, A.
   1990   *The Call to Personhood: A Christian theory of the individual in social relationships*, Cambridge.

Marshall, I.H.
   1978   *The Gospel of Luke*, Exeter.

Morgan, R. (ed.)
   1989   *Religion of the Incarnation: Anglican essays in commemoration of* Lux Mundi, Bristol.

Norris, R.A.
   1966   *God and the World in Early Christian Theology*, London.

Pannenberg, W.
   1968   *Jesus: God and Man*, London.
   1972   *The Apostles' Creed*, London.

Peacock, A. and Gillett, G. (eds.)
   1976   *Persons and Personality*, Oxford.

Pollard, T.E.
   1970   *Johannine Christology and the Early Church*, Cambridge.

Race, A.
   1993   *Christians and Religious Pluralism*, 2nd edn, London.

Rahner, K.
   1966   *Investigations*, vol. 5, London.

Ramsey, A.M.
   1961   *The Resurrection of Christ*, Glasgow.

Robinson, J.A.T.
   1963   *Honest to God*, London.

Rowland, C. and Fletcher-Lois, C.H.T. (eds.)
   1998   *Understanding, Studying and Reading: New Testament eassays in honour of John Ashton*, Sheffield 1998.

Rudolph, K.
   1983   *Gnosis: The nature and history of an ancient religion*, trans. R. McL. Wilson, Edinburgh. 1st edn, Leipzig, 1977.

Sanders, E.P.
   1985   *Jesus and Judaism*, London.

Schillebeeckx, E.
   1979   *Jesus: An experiment in Christology*, London.

Schürer, E.
   1979   *The History of the Jewish People in the Age of Jesus Christ*, vol. ii, revd and ed. G. Vermes, F. Millar and M. Black, Edinburgh.

Spong, J.S.
   1994   *Resurrection, Myth or Reality?*, San Francisco.

Stevenson, J. (ed.)
   1966   *Councils, Creeds, and Controversies*, London.

Taylor, C.
   1989   *Sources of the Self: The making of modern identity*, Cambridge.

Tillich, P.
  1963 *Christianity and the Encounter with World Religions*, New York and London.
  1978 *Systematic Theology*, vols. i and ii, London.
Trompf, G.W. and Hamel, G. (eds.)
  2002 *The World of Religions: Essays on historical and contemporary issues*, Dehli.
Vermes, G.
  1973 *Jesus the Jew*, London.
  1975 *The Dead Sea Scrolls in English*, 2nd edn, Harmondsworth.
  1977 *The Dead Sea Scrolls*, London.
Wallace-Hadrill, D.S.
  1982 *Christian Antioch*, Cambridge.
Wickham, L.R.
  1983 *Cyril of Alexandria: Select letters*, Oxford.
Williams, T.S.M.
  1985 *Form and Vitality in the World and God*, Oxford.
Whiteley, D.E.H.
  1964 *The Theology of St Paul*, Oxford.
Wiles, M.F.
  1967 *The Making of Christian Doctrine*, Cambridge.
  1976 *Working Papers in Doctrine*, London.
  1977 *Myth in Theology*, in J. Hick (ed.) *The Myth of God Incarnate*, London.
Wilken, R.L.
  1984 *The Christians as the Romans saw them*, New Haven and London.
Wright, N.T.
  1992 *Who was Jesus?*, London.
Young, F.
  1975 *Sacrifice and Death of Christ*, London.
  1983 *From Nicaea to Chalcedon*, London.
Zahrnt, H.
  1965 *The Question of God: Protestant theology in the twentieth century*, transln, London.

Index of Modern Authors

Badham, P. 71
Barth, K. 138 ff., 148 f.
Pope Benedict XVI 3
Berger, P. 39, 61
Bultmann, R. 56 f.

Carnley, P. 76, 82
Cupitt, D. 11

Darwin, C. 53
Dunn, J.D.G. 97

Fenton, J. 83
Feuerbach, L. 8

Harnack, A. von 138
Harré, R. 8, 13 ff, 16, 19, 27
Harvey, A.E. 78, 81
Hebblethwaite, P. 82
Heidegger, M. 56 f.
Hengel, M. 38 f.
Hick, J. 11, 143
Houlden, J.L. 76, 79, 82

Jansz, J. 8, 15, 27
Pope John Paul II 141

Küng, H. 142

Lampe, G.W.H. 96

Lindars, B. 78f., 82
Lyttleton, A. 49 f.
McFadyen, A. 8
Marx, K. 58
Morgan, R. 76, 81
Moule, C.F.D. 71
Muddiman, J. 72
Murray and Stein 12

Pannenenberg, W. 74, 79
Pope Pius IX 145, 149

Rahner, K. 141, 149
Rowland, C. 72, 80

Sanders, E.P. 32, 43
Schillebeeckx, E. 77
Selby, P.S.M. 84
Shotter, J. 9
Spong, J. 77, 79, 83
Strauss, D. 79

Tillich, P. 1, 2, 17, 56, 77, 79, 83, 142, 148 f.

Watson, F. 79 f.
Westcott, B.F. 71, 79
Wright, N.T. 78, 83

Young, F. 34

Biblical quotations are from the Revised Standard Version unless stated otherwise.

General Index

Adam and Eve 50, 60
Agnostics 63. Cf. p. 153
Alexandria/Alexandrians 104 f. 109, 116, 129
Alienation 21, 56, 59 ff., 62 ff.
Antioch/Antiochenes 104 f., 108, 115 f., 118, 129
Apocalyptic 80, 83
Apologists 102
Apollinaris 119
Aristotle 58, 99
Arius/Arianism 103, 106, 109, 129
Ascension 5, 76
Athanasius 110, 118
Atonement 38 f., 49 ff., 51 f., 56, 61
  Day of 31 ff.
Authentic/inauthentic 56 f., 60, 68
Authority 41, 59, 60 f., 88, 93, 96, 114, 137
Autonomy 16, 23

Being/Becoming 90, 99 f.
Ben Sira 34, 96
Bible/Scriptures 23, 58, 105, 118, 122, 144
  Inerrancy 3, 145
  Old Testament 31, 41, 83, 93, 96, 101, 103, 105
  Septuagint 96
Bridge words/beings 91, 96 f., 103

Caesaria Philippi (Peter) 77
Caiaphas 74, 83
Church 4, 15, 21, 42, 89, 142, 146
Clothes 71, 81, 83
Cognitive structures/world views 60, 78
Commitment 3, 5 f., 46, 83, 87, 89, 92, 96, 111 f., 123 f., 128, 154

Constantine 110
Constructionism (*see* Social Constructionism)
Cowboys 54
Creation 22 f., 55, 64, 89 f. 95, 96 f. 99 ff., 101 f.
Creeds
  Constantinople 111 ff.
  Chalcedon 120, 123 f., 129
  Nicaea 110 f. 113
Cyril of Alexandria 117 f., 119

Demonic 23, 26, 54, 59, 69, 143, 145, 148
Demythologization 56
  Existential 54 ff.
  Sociological 58
Devil 13, 52 ff., 57, 63, 65
Docetic/anti-docetic 76, 79, 94, 112
Doctrines 4, 49 ff., 56, 71
Doctrinal pluralism 51
Doctrinal reconstruction 51, 56, 58 ff., 61 f., 67

Ecumenism 3
Existential 9, 42, 54, 57 f.

Faith 46, 54 f., 63, 67 f., 74, 79, 81, 88 f., 104, 108, 127, 130, 145
  Blind faith 55
Faiths/Religions cf. 18, cf. 22, 65, 137, 142
  Copernican revolution 143 ff.
  Exclusivist 138, 140, 144
  Inclusivist 141, 145
  Mystical, Moral, Futurist co-existence 146
  Pluralist 140, 144 ff., 147, 149

169

Index

Universalism 140
Fall 57, 140
Forgiveness 45, 52, 67 ff.
Fundamentalism 1, 5, 65, 145

Gnostics 45, 98
  Marcion 45, 78
God 21, 84, 87, 108, 130, 149
  Father 23, 44, 101 ff., 107, 112 f., 116, 148
  Transcendent/immanent 90 ff., 94

Holy Spirit (Spirit) 5, 84, 88, 93 f., 104, 112, 114, 124, 140
Homoousios 110 f., 117
Hope 53, 67, 69, 77 f., 80, 153
Humanity 8, 23, 26 f., cf. 13, 42, 45, 49 f., 55, 66 f., 78, 84, 93 f. 96

Idols 58, 62 ff.
Incarnation 22, cf. 23, 50, 59, 67, 106, 117, 122, 126, 159.
Individualism 19 f. 25, 35, 58
Infallibility 3
Irenaeus 12 f.

Jesus 1, 14, 41, 49 ff., 50, 54, 56 f., 61 ff., 66, 84, 98, 111; *see* Logos
  Agent of God 89, 125
  Christos 92, 94
  Cross 27, 45, 77, 149
  Death/Crucifixion 62, 87 f., 145
  Definition of God 95, cf. 97
  Form of God 89, 117, 128 f.
  Freedom 61 f., 115, 122
  Friend of sinners 43
  Fulfilment of Scripture 41
  Historical 22, 88, 94 f., 102
  Humanity of 4, 7, 62, 87, 92, 98, 115 f., 119, 122, 128 f.
  Lord 27, 83 f. 92 ff., 129 f.
  Mythological significance 55
  Person of 4, 14, 22, cf. 17, 27.
  Revealer 57, cf. 64, 66, 78, 116, 121, 127, 148

Risen Lord 76, 78, 88, 94, 103, 122
Sinless 127 f.
Son 89 f., 96 f. 113, 116, 122, 125
Son of Man 72
Jews/Judaism 55, 90 f., 95
Justice 137, 144 f., 154

Language 4 ff., 27, 40 f., 51 f., 55, 57, 75, 87, 89, 93, 111 f. 126
  Credal terms (substance, nature, person/*prosopon*) 112, 117, 125
  Confessional/Descriptive 126 128
Law of Moses/Torah 31, 35 f., 38, 42 ff., 53, 61, 66, 89, 96 f.
Liberation 59, 65
Logos 98, 100 f., 125
  Logos and God the Father 102 f., 105, 113, 115, 120, 122, 124
  Logos and Jesus the man 103 ff., 113, 120, 124
  Logos-Son 108 f., 113 ff., 116 f., 120, 124, 129 f.
Love 12, 16 ff., 20 f., 25, 56, 63 f., 68 f., 113, 115, 123, 126, 137, 144 f., 149 f., 154

Maccabees 38, 66
Marxist 58 ff.
Meaning 57, 60, 65, 153
Messiah/Christ 61, 75, 77 f., 90, 92, 95, 104, 121, 125, 130
Middle Platonism 99, 100 ff. 103, 105 f.
Moral Order 10 f., 14
Myth 52 ff., 80
  Reality-constituting story 52, 54
  Demythologization 56
  Deliteralization 56
  Mythological 54, 78, 126, 144

Nazis 18 f.
Nestorius 117
New Testament 23 ff., 93

Objective/Subjective knowledge 87, 92 f., 97

170

Index

Ontological corollary 5, 131

Paul 4, 34, 49, 55, 58, 63, 73, 82 ff., 88, 92, 97 f., 153
Pelagius 16
Pentateuch 41
Person 7, 51, 67 f., 84, 114
Personal being 10, 13 ff., 17 ff., 21 ff.,
Person making 18, 24 f., 68
Personhood/Selfhood 6, 7 ff., 13 ff., 17, 20 ff., 45, 60, 64, 147, 150
  Gift and achievement 12 f., 24 f., 17 f., 20, 22 ff., 27
Philo 35, 103
Plato 58, 99 f.
Plausibility crises 39, 60
Pluralism 1, 7, 8, 11, 13, 26, 49, 137, 149
Postmodern 1, 7, 147
Priest(hood) 33, 41 f., 60, 90
Prophets 34 f. 58, 67, 90, 92, 99, 102
Punishment 4, 52, 66
  Penal substitution 39, 45, 52, 54

Reason 55, 98, 100
Reconciliation 49, 65, 68, 101, 144
Redemption ch. 3 *passim*, 46
Religions 26, 45, 147 f.
Resurrection ch. 4 *passim*, 122
  Biblical problems 72 ff.
  Clothes 71, 76
  Doctrinal problems 74 ff.
  Empty tomb 71, 73, 76 ff., 81
  Galilee 73, 81 ff.
  Women's testimony 82
Revelation 45, 66, 96, 113, 116 f, 139, 148.

Sacrifice ch. 2 *passim*, 66–7
  Animal 41
  Death acceptable to God 45, 66
  Enriched 42
  Martyr death 37
  OT background 31
  Spiritualisation 33, 40
  Vicarious 37

Salvation 57, 59, 137, 140, 142 f.
Satisfaction 52, 54
Science 58
Sin 31 ff., 39, 45, 52, 56, 58, 63, 68, 114, 139
  Rebellion 32 f., 44
  Ritual impurity 32 f., 44
Sincerity 6, 60
Social constructionism 5, 8, 9 ff., 11, 14 ff., 26, cf. 84
  Jesus in the light of 14,
Subjectivism 79 f., 84
Subordinationism 106 f., 114
Suffering 36, 38 f., 45, 52, 109, 121 ff., 130
Symbols 77, 89 ff., 94 f., 97, 106, 108, 111, 122 f., 126
  of transcendence 94, 101 f., 112, 122, 130
  of immanence 90 f., 94

Temple 33 f., 41 f., 43 f., 61, 78
Theodore of Mopsuestia 117
Torah 61, 66, 89, 96 f.
Trinity 5, 23 f., 64, 75, 92, 96, 125, 129 f., 144, 130; *see* Appendix
Truth 51, 53, 56, 60, 127

Ultimacy 1, 3, 26, 67, 87, 95, 113, 144, 148
Ultimacy of Jesus 1, 3 f., 7, 31, 46, 63 f., 80, 83 f., 88 f., 97 f., 101, 105, 108, 110 f., 113, 115, 120 ff., 123, 125, 130 f., 137, 146, 149, 154

Vindication/Exaltation 78, 80 f.
Virginal Conception 14, 75

Wisdom (Sophia) 95 ff., 98, 102, 121 f., 125.
Word 95, 102
Word of God 57 f. 99, 101, 103, 107; *see* Logos

Zacchaeus 44